CW00958397

Miniflashcard
Language Game

FOOTBALL
FEVER!

LANGUAGES THROUGH FOOTBALL
Susan Thomas

PHOTOCOPIABLE SERIES

Football Fever - Languages through Football
Susan Thomas

With thanks to Isabelle Ayma, Christopher Connolly, Carmen Bishton, Salvador Estébanez and José Luis Llamas of the Instituto Cervantes Manchester, Moira Edwards and Arbroath Academy, Elizabeth Evans, Stéphane Foullon, Timothy Hilgenberg, Denise Hobbs, Hilary McColl, David Miller and colleagues and learners of Oldborough Manor Community School, Frauke Noelker, Muriel Offord, Karl Pfeiffer of the Goethe Institute London, Peter Rodgers and colleagues and learners of Swanwick Hall School, Christine Ross and Perth & Kinross Modern Languages Office, Laetitia Sagoo, Paul Sanday, Ivana Stanley, Daniel Vangenechten, Nathalie Vieillard, Frances Walsh.

Illustrations by Heather Clarke.
Cover design by Hannah Berridge.

Football Fever !

1 Introduction

About this book

Have you ever wished for resources which would help you to:

- generate enthusiasm amongst your reluctant adolescents, *and*
- be sufficiently straightforward for them to be successful, *as well as*
- cover the basic syllabus, *and even*
- encourage creative use of language?

You need look no further. This book:

- centres around the topic of football, one of the abiding interests of many of your pupils;
- starts from the language they already know (like *j'aime le football*) but offers them the chance to say much more;
- exploits a rich seam of language, to cover basics like number, time, weather, clothes (all in the context of football); and
- takes your serious enthusiasts through specialist vocabulary and into the realms of creative language, helping them to write appreciations of their favourite players and so on.

How the book is organised

The first two sections of the book contain mostly general language, allowing familiar vocabulary to be re-used in the context of football. There is some football-specific vocabulary and the occasional introduction of some specialist vocabulary where necessary to achieve the purpose of the activity.

The third section also introduces a considerable amount of general vocabulary and structures, but also introduces more specialised topics and word banks needed to allow your high-fliers to experiment with forms of writing which match their interests and, hopefully, their developing skills.

How to use the resources

Do not attempt to use all the material, or to use it in the sequence provided here. Select your activity carefully, and then select the visuals you will need to support that. Individual illustrations can be cut and pasted into the format which will best suit your pupils and the activity you have in mind

2 Suggested activities and games

Many simple games can be played using the resources supplied. Each game framework can be used to prompt words, phrases or sentences. For example, in response to a visual, learners can: name an item, describe an item or scene, suggest what someone may be thinking or saying, and so on.

A list of *Suggested Language* is provided with each set of visuals but these can, of course, be changed to suit the requirements of the class. The suggestions given below cover:
- Whole class work using the OHP.
- Games and activities for groups of 2 - 6 players.

Using the OHP

The OHP is useful for whole class work at various stages in the programme. It can be used for
- reviewing vocabulary previously learned, in order to link it to new vocabulary;
- presenting new vocabulary;
- teacher-led practice of new vocabulary;
- assessing whether new vocabulary has been well-enough learned for the class to proceed to group work;
- playing games in which the whole class can join;
- demonstrating an activity or game which learners are about to carry out in groups;
- organising feedback about an activity;
- assessing the quality of learning which has taken place during group work;
- revising vocabulary at a later stage in the programme.

OHP Activities

- Photocopy visuals onto acetate to create OHP transparencies.
- Move picture items on the OHP slowly into focus for learners to name.
- Reveal sections of picture items bit by bit for learners to name.
- Colour in pictures following learners' instructions.
- Put on overlays for eg prices of items.
- Play simple games eg *What's on the Card ? Noughts and Crosses, Kim's Game, True or False,* or *Guessing Game.*

How to prepare the photocopiable resources

- They can be photocopied on to paper, for use as handouts or worksheets.
- They can be enlarged, for display or for making flashcards.
- They can be copied on to card, perhaps enlarged, and then cut to make individual cards for games and activities.
- Text can be added beneath pictures or on the backs of cards.
- For maximum durability, visuals can be copied on to paper, glued on to thick card and covered with plastic.
- Once copied, visuals can be combined or grouped to make display materials, or used to compile a picture dictionary or topic reference book.
- Blank masters can be used to create new sets of visuals, to make matching text cards and new games.

Suggested Activities and Games

What's Shown on the Card ?   (Cards with text written on the back or checklist of vocabulary)

- **Picture Spread:** Spread the cards picture up over the table. Take it in turns to choose an item and name it. If you are right, take the card. If you are wrong, put the card back. The player with the most cards at the end of the game wins. *(Offers free choice of seen cards.)*
- **Pick a Card:** Fan out some cards for another player to choose and name. If s/he is wrong, the card is put back into the pack. *(Choice of unseen cards.)*
- **Guess the Card:** Place a small number of cards face down. Players in turn guess (or take bets on) which one is on the top. *(Choice of unseen cards. Winning based more on luck than knowledge.)*
- **Take that Card:**   Place the cards in the middle of the table. Take it in turns to name the item on the top card. If you are wrong, the card goes to the bottom of the pack. *(No choice of card.)*
- **Quick Flash:** The quizperson holds up a card for one second only. The first player to name the item shown wins the card. *(No choice of card. Competitive. Time pressure.)*

Line Solitaire

Lay out some cards in a line. Name the first item. Then check the answer. If you are right, you carry on. If you get one wrong, then you try and learn it. Then turn all the cards back over, and start again. The aim is to find your longest run without any mistakes. From time to time you can shuffle the cards. (You can also play this in pairs or teams.)

Noughts and Crosses   (9 cards or section of picture board)

Lay out the cards 3 x 3 on the table. Take it in turns to name an item. If you are right, turn the card over, or place a coloured counter on the board. The next player names an item. If s/he is correct, the card is turned over and placed sideways or a different coloured counter is placed on the board. Three cards in a row wins the game.

Beat the Clock

Name as many items as possible within a time limit eg souvenirs, or names of the World Cup countries.

I Spy....

Spread out some cards picture up over the table. Call out the beginning letter of an item for the other players to find. The first person to give the name of the correct item keeps the card and becomes the next quizperson.

Kim's Game

Spread out some cards over the table. One of you removes a card while the others turn away. They then look at the cards. The first player to name the missing item wins a point.

Matching Pairs   (2 sets of cards)

Spread out the two sets of pictures face down on the table. Turn over two at a time to see if they match, naming the items as you do so. If they match, name the item correctly and take the cards.
DIY Matching Pairs: Write a word, phrase or sentence about each picture on slips of paper. The next group matches up the pictures and sentences.
Variation 1: Match some phrases to pictures of fans, players, coach etc - what are each of them saying?
Variation 2: Match players to teams/countries.
Variation 3: Match player to item they endorse/advertise eg *shampoo, pizza, trainers* etc!

Snap (4 sets of cards)

Shuffle the cards and deal them out. You each in turn play a card. If one card played is the same as the previous one, the first person to call out the name of the item gets the cards.

Happy Families (4 sets of cards)

Shuffle the cards and deal them out. The aim is to collect sets of items. If, for example, you already have two 'shirts' in your hand, you ask another player *Have you got a shirt?* If s/he has, s/he gives you the card in return for one you wish to discard. The first player to collect complete sets of 4 wins.
Variation 1: DIY Happy Families - collect players from eg the same club/country.
Variation 2: DIY Happy Families - learners colour in Kit in different colours and collect sets.

3 in a Row   (Any picture board)

Choose a picture square and name an item in it, or say something about the picture. If you are right, put a counter on the square. The first player to get three counters in a row wins.
Variation: Using MiniFlashcard 12 Sided Dice or Spinner. As above, but throw the dice first to pinpoint a square.

Bingo   (Any picture board)

Choose 8 items from the 12 on a picture board and put a cross in one corner of each of the 8 squares. The quizperson calls out the 12 items in any order. If you have marked one of the items called out, you put a counter on the square. The first player to cover all their marked squares calls out an agreed word.

Charades   (Any cards)

Take a picture card. Mime an item eg person - *player, manager, fan, commentator* for others to guess.
Variation: Make up and use text cards as prompts instead of picture cards.

Simon Says (Selected cards)

The leader uses the pictures to prompt instructions. Example: *Stand up, kick, throw, hold up a card.*

I Went to Market...

Spread some cards out on the table. One of you starts a sentence. Each player adds an item. Example:
I went to the souvenir shop and bought a programme.., a video etc.
During the match, X scored a goal.., Y committed a foul.., X got a penalty etc.
In my Dream Team I would have X as goalkeeper.., Y as a striker.., Z as a defence etc.
In the First Aid Kit there's a sponge.., a bandage.., a spray etc.

Guessing Game (Any picture board)

Describe one of the pictures. The other players guess which one it is.
You wear them on your feet. (boots)   The referee has one in his pocket. (book)

True or False   (Any picture board)

The teacher or learner describes a picture. For example (Verbs - Fans - Unit 20)*In Picture No 3 the fan is eating a burger. (False)*
If you are the first player to call out *True* or *False* correctly, you get a point.
Variation: The teacher or learner reads out a list of statements. You jot down which are *True* and which are *False*. Check answers at the end.

20 Questions

Players have 20 questions to guess a player eg what nationality, what club, what position, how old, what colour hair..

Battleship Buddies (9 selected cards)

Lay out 9 picture items in a 3 x 3 grid behind a book so your partner cannot see them. Say which items you have and where they are. The other player has to put his/her pictures in the right place. For example:
The shirt is on the top shelf. Put the postcards on the middle shelf between the videos and the programmes.
Variation: Draw pictures instead of placing cards.
Variation: Put players in position in a Dream Team.

DIY Odd One Out

Make up groups of prompts for others to guess the odd one out. For example:
Players - from different clubs/leagues/countries.

Story Telling

Deal a few cards of mixed titles at random eg Weather, Fans' Verbs, Moods and make up a short sequence or story.

Dice Games

NB: MiniFlashcard Language Games produce a range of dice: Question, Pronoun, Tenses, Colour, Mood and Number. These can be introduced as an extra prompt with many of the above games.

Other Activities

Songs/Chants/Poems

- Find and listen to French Club Football Chants on the Internet. Or Make up your own French chants/variations on existing chants. Examples:
  Oh là, Oh là, Oh là là
  En Europe à petits pas
  Quand on y est
  On va chanter
  Le RFC
  La Coupe aurait !

- *Debout si tu détestes (+ nom de l'équipe adverse* - name of opposing team)
- Or rhythm clap, say player's name at the end.
- Compose a Valentine's card or Christmas card to your favourite team.

TV/Videos

If you can obtain French football videos, or record prgrammes from the TV - use them to model and practise football commentaries. Pause videos where appropriate to comment on/describe the action, or what players/fans are wearing/look like/saying/thinking.

Video Cameras

Record your own sports programme post-match commentaries, and mock interviews of personalities, football apprentices, or managers after a match. Shoot a sequence on the pitch, in the changing room or gym, with commentary. Do action replays - was it a handball, was the referee right to award that penalty? Did the player fall in the box or was he tripped?

Language Assistants

If you have access to a foreign language assistant...

Prepare tapes so learners can match the information to pictures or include it in charts. For example:
- Football results - draw up a chart - learners fill in the results as they come in (not in the same order as on the chart).
- Weather reports.
- A sequence of events on the pitch - put picture cards in the correct order.
- Dream Team selections.

Coin Football/Fanzine Corner

Use French football magazines for information about players, teams, and events.
Keep a display including for example:
- Topical news items.
- Newspaper/magazine clippings.
- Newspaper headlines on the class's favourite team or event.
- Results - use desk top publishing to draw up bar charts.
- Dream team of the week.
- Chant/Rhyme of the week.
- A display showing the number of days to go to the World Cup, or other event.

Surf the Net

For information on players, teams, and events.

3 Football and Me!

SUGGESTED LANGUAGE:

English	French	German	Spanish
Do you like football?	Tu aimes le foot?	Magst du Fußball?	¿Te gusta el fútbol?
Do you play football?	Tu joues au foot?	Spielst du Fußball?	¿Juegas al fútbol?
Where?	Où?	Wo?	¿Dónde?
In the garden?	Dans le jardin?	Im Garten?	¿En el jardín?
At school?	A l'école?	In der Schule?	¿En la escuela?
At the stadium?	Au stade?	Im Stadion?	¿En el estadio?
In the park?	Au parc?	Im Park?	¿En el parque?
On the beach?	A la plage?	Am Strand?	¿En la playa?
When?	Quand?	Wann?	¿Cuándo?
At the weekend?	Le week-end?	Am Wochenende?	¿(En) el fin de semana?
On Saturdays?	Le samedi?	Samstags?	¿Los sábados?
Every Saturday?	Tous les samedis?	Jeden Samstag?	¿Cada sábado?
On Saturday mornings?	Le samedi matin?	Samstag vormittag?	¿Los sábados por la mañana?
In winter?	En hiver?	Im Winter?	¿En (el) invierno?
In summer?	En été?	Im Sommer?	¿En (el) verano?
In the holidays?	Pendant les vacances?	In den Ferien?	¿En (las) vacaciones?
When the weather's nice?	Quand il fait beau?	Wenn es schön ist?	¿Cuándo el tiempo es bueno?
When it rains?	Quand il pleut?	Wenn es regnet?	¿Cuándo llueve?
When it snows?	Quand il neige?	Wenn es schneit?	¿Cuándo nieva?
Who with?	Avec qui?	Mit wem?	¿Con quién?
With your friends?	Avec tes copains/copines?	Mit deinen Freunden /Freundinnen?	¿Con tus amigos?
What do you wear?	Qu'est-ce que tu portes?	Was hast du an?	¿Qué llevas puesto?
A football shirt?	Un maillot de foot?	Ein Trikot/Hemd?	¿Una camiseta de fútbol?
Football boots?	Des chaussures de foot?	Fußballschuhe/stiefel?	¿Botas de fútbol?
What do you drink?	Qu'est-ce que tu bois?	Was trinkst du?	¿Qué bebes?
Coke?	Un coca?	Cola?	¿Coca cola?
Lemonade?	De la limonade?	Sprudel/Limonade?	¿Limonada?
What do you eat?	Qu'est-ce que tu manges?	Was ißt du?	¿Qué comes?
An orange?	Une orange?	Eine Orange?	¿Una naranja?
A banana?	Une banane?	Eine Banane?	¿Un plátano?
Do you play in a team?	Tu joues dans une équipe?	Spielst du in einer Mannschaft / in einem Verein?	¿Juegas en un equipo?
What position?	Quelle position?	Auf / In welcher Position?	¿En qué posición?
Why do you like that position?	Pourquoi aimes-tu cette position?	Warum gefällt dir diese Position?	¿De qué juegas? ¿Por qué te gusta esa posición?
I like to...score goals!	J'aime..marquer des buts!	Ich schieße gerne Tore!	¡Me gusta marcar goles!
What are your team colours?	Quelles sont vos couleurs?	Was sind deine Mannschaftsfarben?	¿Cuáles son los colores de tu equipo?
Do you win often?	Vous gagnez souvent?	Gewinnt ihr oft?	¿Ganáis a menudo?
Which team do you support?	Tu es supporter /supportrice de quelle équipe?	Für welche Mannschaft bist du?	¿Cuál es tu equipo? ¿De qué equipo eres?
I support Newcastle United.	Je suis supporter /supportrice du Newcastle United.	Ich bin Newcastle United Fan.	Soy aficionado/a del Newcastle United.

SUGGESTED ACTIVITIES:

- Selected activities from Unit 2, eg Kim's Game.
- Use pictures to prompt questions and answers. Number picture items and roll one or two six-sided dice to pinpoint a particular picture.

Football and Me

4   My Favourite Player (A)

Mon joueur favori

SUGGESTED LANGUAGE:

Name:	Nom:	Name:	Nombre:
Date of Birth:	Né:	Geboren:	Fecha de nacimiento:
Place of Birth:	A:	In:	Lugar de nacimiento:
Nationality:	Nationalité:	Staatsangehörigkeit:	Nacionalidad:
Age:	Age:	Alter:	Edad:
Height:	Taille:	Größe:	Altura:
Weight:	Poids:	Gewicht:	Peso:
Colour of hair:	Couleur des cheveux:	Haarfarbe:	Color del pelo:
Colour of eyes:	Couleur des yeux:	Augenfarbe:	Color de ojos:
Favourite music:	Musique favorite:	Lieblingsmusik:	Música favorita:
Favourite food:	Repas favori:	Lieblingsessen/speise:	Comida favorita:
Favourite holidays:	Vacances favorites:	Lieblingsferien:	Vacaciones favoritas:
Favourite clothes:	Vêtements favoris:	Lieblingskleidung:	Ropa favorita:
Favourite sport:	Sport favori:	Lieblingssport:	Deporte favorito:
Favourite pet:	Animal favori:	Lieblingstier:	Mascota favorita:
Favourite car:	Voiture favorite:	Lieblingsauto:	Coche favorito:
Position:	Poste:	Position:	Posición:
Club:	Club:	Verein:	Club:
Stadium:	Stade:	Stadion:	Estadio:
Honours:	Palmarès:	Auszeichnungen:	Palmarés / Galardones / Trofeos:
I like:	J'aime:	Ich mag:	
I love:	J'adore:	Ich liebe:	Me gusta:
Verdict:	Verdict:	Fazit:	Me encanta:
			Opinión / Veredicto:

SUGGESTED ACTIVITIES:

- Selected activities from Unit 2.
- Talk about your favourite player. Include the information suggested above, or anything else you'd like to say. You can make up any details you do not know!
- Link to the sections on favourite players in Units 51-53.

My Favourite Player

5　Weather

La météo

This is a very important factor in terms of its impact on the standard/style of play, clothing, and advantages to different teams used to playing in different climatic conditions and on different pitches! Fans, players, and managers look anxiously at the weather forecast .

SUGGESTED LANGUAGE:

1. it's hot
2. it's cold
3. it's sunny
4. it's windy
5. it's foggy
6. it's freezing
7. it's raining
8. it's snowing
9. it's cloudy

1. il fait chaud
2. il fait froid
3. il fait du soleil/il y a du soleil
4. il fait du vent/il y a du vent
5. il fait du brouillard/il y a du brouillard
6. il gèle
7. il pleut
8. il neige
9. il y a des nuages/ letemps est couvert

1. es ist warm/heiß
2. es ist kalt
3. es ist sonnig/die Sonne scheint
4. es ist windig
5. es ist nebelig
6. es friert/es ist eisig
7. es regnet
8. es schneit
9. es ist bewölkt

1. hace calor
2. hace frío
3. hace sol
4. hace viento
5. hay niebla
6. está helando
7. está lloviendo
8. está nevando
9. está nublado

ADDITIONAL LANGUAGE:

1. la météo
2. quel temps fait-il aujourd'hui?
3. il fait beau
4. il fait mauvais
5. il fera beau/il va faire beau aujourd'hui
6. il va pleuvoir cet après-midi
7. une averse
8. un orage
9. la boue
10. quelle équipe sera inquiète? contente?
11. l'arbitre peut interdire un match s'il juge que le terrain est dangereux (trous, gel, boue épaisse, neige)

1. the weather forecast
2. what's the weather like today?
3. it's fine, it's a nice day
4. the weather's bad
5. it's going to be a nice day
6. it's going to rain this afternoon
7. a downpour
8. a storm
9. mud
10. which team will be worried? happy?
11. the referee can cancel a match if s/he considers that the ground is dangerous (potholes, ice, thick mud, snow)

SUGGESTED ACTIVITIES:

- Selected activities from Unit 2.
- Practise tenses.
- What's the weather like today - is it nice for playing football?
- Make up weather reports for match locations, including the temperature.

Manchester:	12 degrés	Il y a du soleil	12 degrees	It's sunny
Paris:	16 degrés	Il pleut	16 degrees	It's raining

- What was the weather like for key matches last weekend?
- Weather chart for Coin Football.
- Link Weather - clothes - players and spectators.

Weather

6 Transport

Le transport

Getting to the match - often a problem!

SUGGESTED LANGUAGE:

1. I walk
2. I go by bus/
   I get the bus
3. I go on the coach
4. I go by car/
   I take the car
5. I go by train/
   I get the train
6. I go on my bike/
   I take my bike
7. I go by taxi/
   I get a taxi
8. I go on my
   motorbike/
   I take my motorbike
9. I go by air/plane/
   I fly
10. I go by boat/on the
    ferry/I get the ferry
11. I go on the
    hovercraft
12. I get the
    underground/tube

1. je vais à pied
2. je vais en autobus/
   je prends le bus
3. je prends le car
4. je vais en voiture
5. je prends le train
6. je vais à vélo
7. je vais en taxi
8. je vais en moto
9. je vais en avion
10. je vais en bateau/je
    prends le ferry
11. je prends
    l'aéroglisseur
12. je prends le métro

1. Ich gehe zu Fuß
2. Ich fahre mit dem
   Bus/
   nehme den Bus
3. Ich fahre mit dem
   (Reise)bus/nehme
   den (Reise)bus
4. Ich fahre mit dem
   Auto/
   nehme das Auto
5. Ich fahre mit dem
   Zug/
   nehme den Zug
6. Ich fahre mit dem
   Fahrrad
7. Ich fahre mit dem
   Taxi/
   nehme ein Taxi
8. Ich fahre mit dem
   Motorrad/nehme
   das Motorrad
9. Ich fliege mit dem
   Flugzeug/nehme
   das Flugzeug
10. Ich fahre mit der
    Fähre/
    nehme die Fähre
11. Ich fahre mit dem
    Luftkissenboot
12. Ich nehme die
    U-Bahn

1. camino
2. voy en autobús/
   cojo el autobús
3. voy en autocar
4. voy en coche/
   cojo el coche
5. voy en tren/
   cojo el tren
6. voy en bici
7. voy en taxi/
   cojo un taxi
8. voy en moto
9. voy en avión/vuelo
10. voy en barco en
    ferry/cojo el barco
11. voy en
    aerodeslizador
12. cojo el metro

ADDITIONAL LANGUAGE:

1. le car des joueurs
2. une ambulance
3. comment allez-vous au match?
4. ça coûte combien?
5. les lignes de métro sont bloquées
6. le bus/train a du retard
7. il y a un embouteillage
8. les routes sont saturées les jours de match
9. le parking n'est pas assez grand

1. the players' coach
2. an ambulance
3. how do you get to the match?
4. how much does it cost?
5. the underground is packed
6. the bus/train is late
7. there's a traffic jam
8. the roads are jammed on match days
9. the car park isn't big enough

SUGGESTED ACTIVITIES:
- Selected games from Unit 2.
- Practise tenses.
- Where do you play football - how do you get there?
- How do you travel to away matches for school/your local team?
- How do you get from where you live to your nearest football stadium?
- Imagine/Describe a journey to a recent away match. What time did you get up? How did you travel? What was the journey like? What time did you get home? How much did it cost?
- How will you get to a World Cup game from where you live?

Transport

7　At the Stadium

Au stade

SUGGESTED LANGUAGE:

1. stadium	1. le stade	1. das Stadion	1. el estadio
2. car park	2. le parking	2. der Parkplatz	2. el aparcamiento
3. ticket office	3. la billetterie/le	3. der Kartenverkauf	3. la taquilla
4. turnstile	guichet	4. das Drehkreuz	4. el torniquete
5. stairs/staircase	4. le tourniquet	5. eine Treppe	5. las escaleras
6. seat	5. un escalier	6. der Sitzplatz	6. una plaza/
7. giant screen	6. le siège/la place	7. eine	un asiento
8. snack bar	7. un écran géant	Riesenleinwand	7. la pantalla gigante
9. toilets	8. la buvette	8. die Snackbar/	8. la cafetería
10. shop	9. les toilettes f	der Kiosk	9. los servicios
11. changing rooms	10. la boutique	9. die Toiletten f	10. la tienda
12. tunnel	11. les vestiaires m	10. der Laden/	11. los vestuarios
	12. le tunnel	der Fanshop	12. el túnel
		11. die Umkleideräume	
		12. der Tunnel	

ADDITIONAL LANGUAGE:

1. l'entrée f	1. entrance
2. la sortie	2. exit
3. la zone (secteur Nord, Sud, Est et Ouest)	3. zone (North, South, East, West)
4. la porte d'accès A-Z	4. entrance A-Z
5. accès ambulance/réservé aux véhicules d'urgence	5. ambulances/emergency vehicles only
6. la tribune	6. stand
7. la loge privée	7. private/corporate box
8. le PC sécurité/les caméras de sécurité	8. security cameras
9. le grillage de protection	9. the security fence
10. le tableau d'affichage	10. scoreboard
11. les douches f	11. showers
12. le bar	12. bar
13. l'ascenseur m	13. lift
14. la cabine téléphonique	14. telephone (box)
15. l'éclairage m	15. floodlights
16. l'infirmerie f	16. medical room/sick bay

SUGGESTED ACTIVITIES:

- Selected games from Unit 2.
- Research some information about a stadium: Example:

Stade:	**Old Trafford**
Club résident:	Manchester United
Capacité actuelle:	56,387 spectateurs
Date de mise en service:	22 janvier 1910
Record de spectateurs:	76,962 (1939 demi-finale FA Cup)
Grands événements:	Coupe du Monde 1966

Nombre de bars/buvettes, ascenseurs, écrans, boutiques?

Places réservées aux handicapés, places pour la presse, places dans les parkings?

Number of bars, snack bars, lifts, screens, shops?

Number of seats reserved for orange badge holders/the disabled, the press, number of spaces in the car parks?

- Mark on the map of France the World Cup Stadia. Research and compare details about them.

At the Stadium

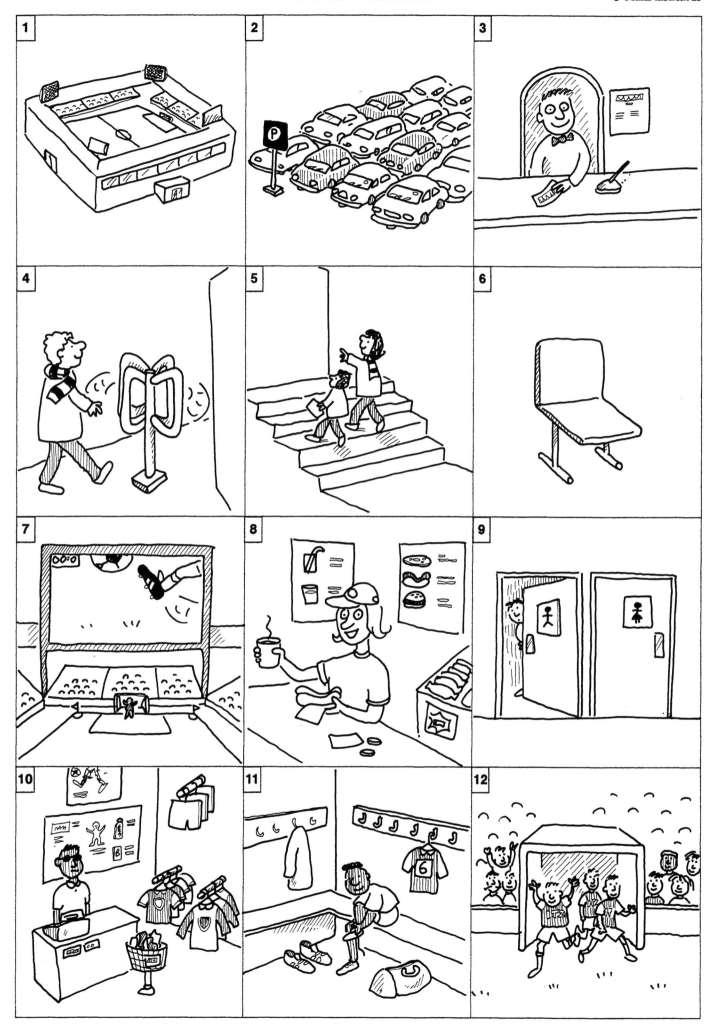

8   Stadium Plan

Le plan du stade

SUGGESTED LANGUAGE:

See previous sheets.

SUGGESTED ACTIVITIES:

- Selected activities from Unit 2, eg I Spy, Beat the Clock.
- Copy or draw a picture of the stadium. Label the key features.
- Describe where things are.
- Compare it to a stadium where your favourite team plays.
- What can you do there? Link to Unit 20 - Fans' Verbs.

Stadium

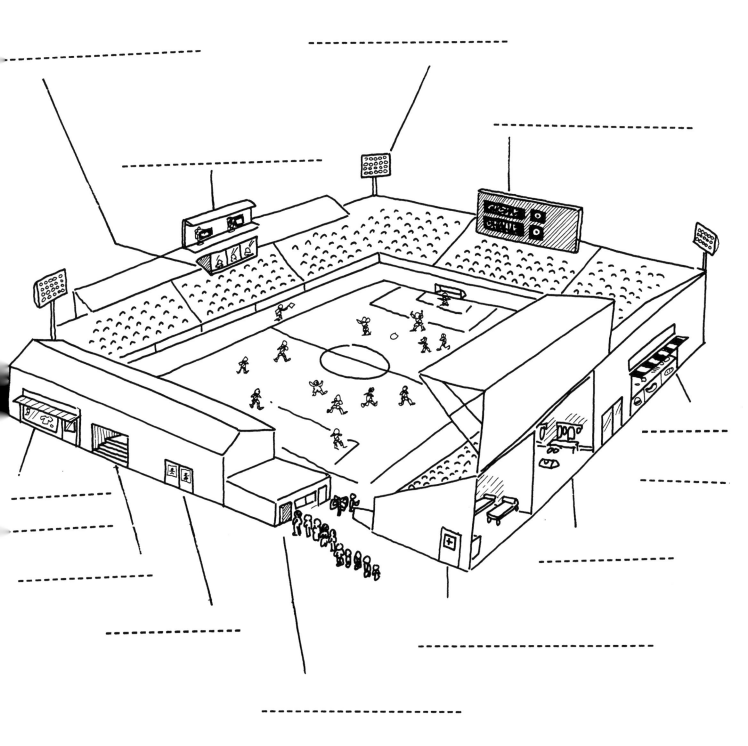

9 Fans' Food

La nourriture des fans

SUGGESTED LANGUAGE:

1. a hotdog	1. un hotdog	1. eine Bockwurst/ ein Hotdog	1. un perrito caliente
2. a burger	2. un hamburger	2. eine Frikadelle/ ein Hamburger	2. una hamburguesa
3. crisps	3. des chips m	3. Chips m	3. patatas fritas
4. a sandwich	4. un sandwich	4. ein Brot/Sandwich	4. un bocadillo
5. a pie	5. un pâté en croûte	5. eine Fleischpastete	5. un empanada
6. chips	6. des frites f	6. Fritten (Pommes frites) pl	6. patatas fritas
7. chocolate	7. du chocolat	7. Schokolade f	7. el chocolate
8. sweets	8. des bonbons m	8. Bonbons/ Süßigkeiten f	8. caramelos
9. an ice-cream	9. une glace	9. ein Eis n	9. un helado
10. a coke	10. un coca	10. eine Cola	10. una coca cola
11. a beer/lager	11. une bière	11. ein Bier	11. una cerveza
12. tea	12. un thé	12. ein Tee	12. un té

ADDITIONAL LANGUAGE:

1. un croque-monsieur	1. toastie
2. un viandox	2. bovril
3. c'est bon?	3. is it nice?
4. c'est délicieux	4. it's delicious
5. c'est dégoûtant	5. it's disgusting
6. ça fait grossir	6. it's fattening
7. le snack préféré des supporters est..	7. the fans' favourite snack is..

SUGGESTED ACTIVITIES:

Selected activities from Unit 2.
- Matching Pairs - Food and Mood/Opinion Spinner.
- DIY Matching Pairs - Food and Prices.

Fans' Food

10 Footballers' Diet

La nourriture des joueurs

SUGGESTED LANGUAGE:

1. des fruits m	1. fruit	1. Obst n	1. la fruta
2. des légumes m	2. vegetables	2. Gemüse n	2. las verduras
3. de la salade	3. salad	3. Salat m	3. la ensalada
4. un bifteck	4. steak	4. ein Steak n	4. el bistec
5. du poisson	5. fish	5. Fisch m	5. el pescado
6. du poulet	6. chicken	6. Hühnchen n	6. el pollo
7. des spaghettis m	7. spaghetti	7. Spaghetti/Nudeln	7. los espaguetis
8. du fromage	8. cheese	8. Käse m	8. el queso
9. du pain	9. bread	9. Brot n	9. el pan
10. des céréales f	10. cereal	10. Cerealien f	10. los cereales
11. du lait	11. milk	11. Milch f	11. la leche
12. un jus d'orange	12. orange juice	12. Orangensaft m	12. el zumo de naranja

ADDITIONAL LANGUAGE:

1. de l'eau minérale f	1. mineral water
2. une banane	2. banana
3. des pâtes f	3. pasta
4. du riz	4. rice
5. des vitamines f	5. vitamins
6. de la nourriture saine	6. healthy food
7. Quand il fait très chaud, les joueurs doivent boire beaucoup pour éviter les crampes et la déshydratation.	7. When it's very hot, the players have to drink a lot to prevent cramp and dehydration.

SUGGESTED ACTIVITIES:

Selected activities from Unit 2.
- Matching Pairs - Food and Mood/Opinion Spinner.
- DIY Matching Pairs - Food and Prices.
- Combine selected Fans' and Footballers' Food pictures. Make up a version of Happy Families. The winner is the one who ends up with a set of healthy food items.

Footballers' Diet

11   Food Role-Play

SUGGESTED LANGUAGE:

A *Hi.*	A *Bonjour.*	A *Hallo.*	A *Hola.*
B *Hi.*	B *Bonjour.*	B *Hallo.*	B *Hola.*
A *Can I help you?*	A *Vous désirez?*	A *Was darf's sein?*	A *¿Qué desea?*
B *Yes, I'd like a hamburger, please.*	B *Un hamburger, s'il vous plaît.*	B *Einen Hamburger, bitte.*	B *Una hamburguesa, por favor.*
A *Anything to drink?*	A *Oui, et comme boisson?*	A *Und zum Trinken?*	A *¿Para beber?*
B *A coke, please.*	B *Un coca, s'il vous plaît.*	B *Eine Cola, bitte.*	B *Una coca cola.*
A *Here you are.*	A *Voilà.*	A *Bitte sehr.*	A *Aquí tiene.*
B *How much is that?*	B *C'est combien?*	B *Wieviel macht das?*	B *¿Cuánto es?*
A *X pounds/pence.*	A *X francs.*	A *X Mark/Pfennig.*	A *X pesetas.*
B *Here you are.*	B *Voilà.*	B *Danke und auf Wiedersehen.*	B *Gracias, hasta luego.*
A *Thank you. Goodbye.*	A *Merci, et au revoir.*	A *Danke, tschüs.*	A *Gracias, hasta luego.*
B *Thank you. Goodbye.*	B *Merci. Au revoir.*		

SUGGESTED ACTIVITY:

- Cut the picture Role Play into two Sections A and B. Two learners act out the roles of A, the food cart assistant, and B, the fan. A third learner can be provided with a sample dialogue as above, and act as observer/prompter.
- Use as a model for additional roleplays.

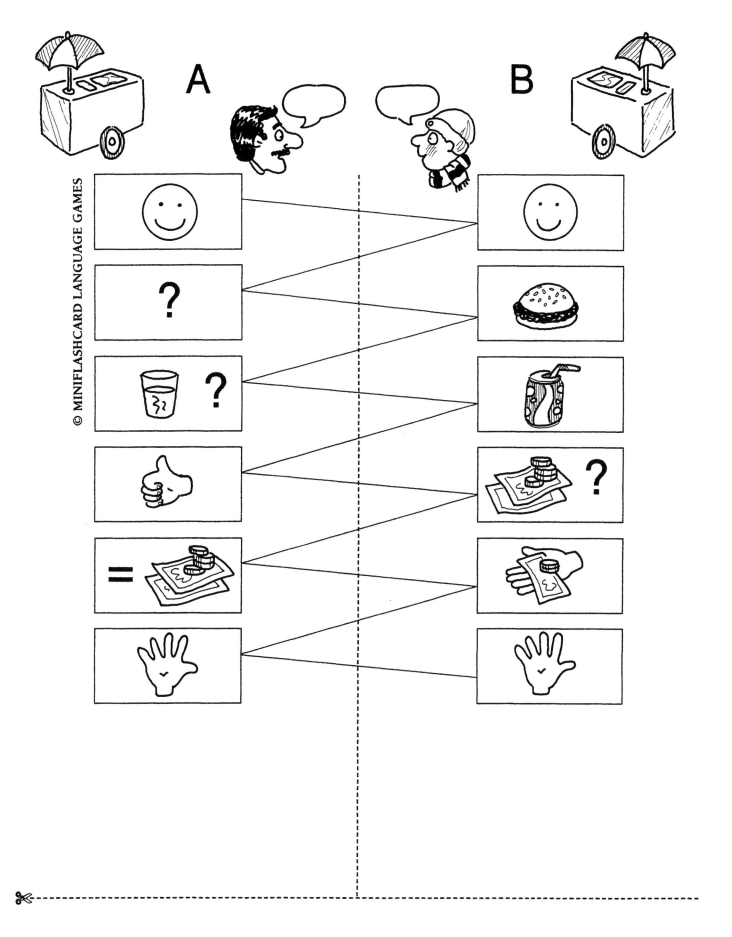

12　Souvenirs

Dans la boutique du supporter

SUGGESTED LANGUAGE:

1. (official) poster
2. programme
3. key ring
4. cap
5. signed football
6. T-shirt
7. video
8. scarf
9. football pen
10. calendar
11. trophy/cup
12. diary

1. un poster (officiel)/ une affiche (officielle)
2. un programme
3. un porte-clés
4. une casquette
5. un ballon dédicacé
6. un T-shirt
7. une cassette vidéo
8. une écharpe
9. un stylo ballon
10. un calendrier
11. un trophée/ unecoupe
12. un agenda

1. ein (offizielles) Poster
2. ein Programm
3. ein Schlüsselanhänger
4. eine Mütze
5. ein signierter Fußball
6. ein T-shirt
7. ein Video
8. ein Schal
9. ein Fußballstift
10. ein Kalender
11. ein Pokal
12. ein Taschenkalender

1. un póster (oficial)
2. una programa
3. un llavero
4. una gorra
5. un balón firmado
6. una camiseta
7. un video
8. una bufanda
9. un bolígrafo de fútbol
10. un calendario
11. un trofeo/una copa
12. una agenda

SUGGESTED ACTIVITIES:

- Selected activities from Unit 2.
- DIY Matching Pairs - Souvenirs and Prices

Souvenirs

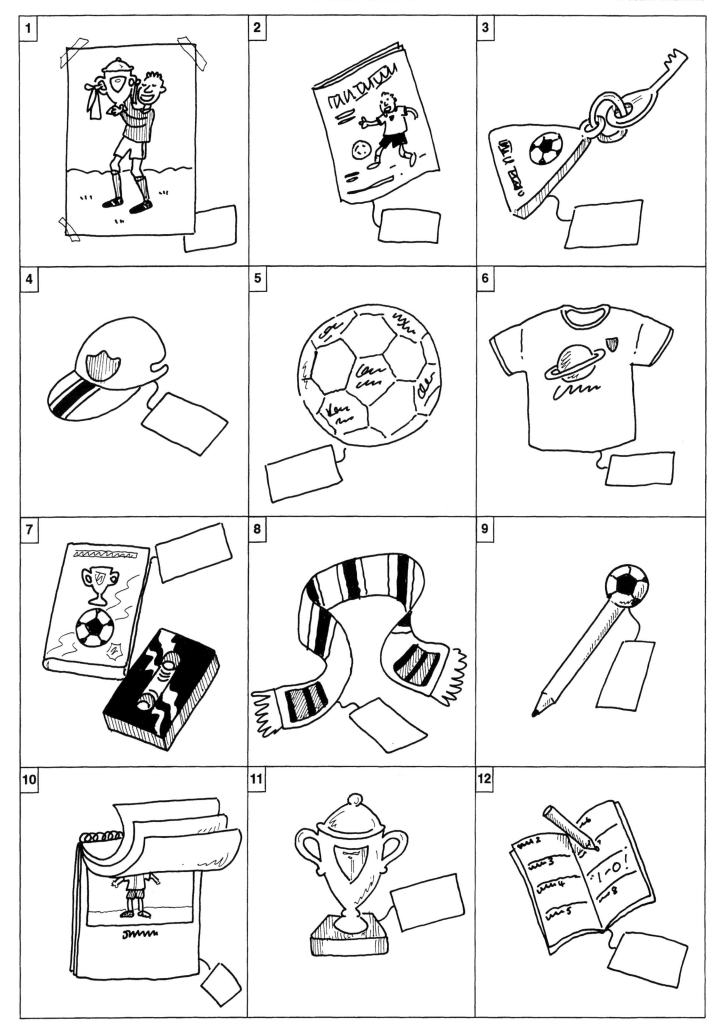

13 More Souvenirs

SUGGESTED LANGUAGE:

1. signed mug
2. sports watch
3. pennant
4. pencil case
5. umbrella
6. ruler
7. CD
8. shield pin
9. car mini kit
10. pack of cards
11. flag
12. supporters' make-up

1. un mugg/une tasse dédicacé(e)
2. une montre (de) sport
3. un fanion
4. une trousse
5. un parapluie
6. une règle
7. un CD
8. un pins blason
9. un mini maillot voiture
10. un jeu de cartes
11. un drapeau
12. le maquillage (du) supporter

1. ein signierter Becher
2. eine Sports-(armband)uhr
3. ein Wimpel m
4. eine Federmappe
5. ein Schirm m
6. ein Lineal n
7. eine CD
8. eine Trophäen-Anstecknadel
9. ein Minidreß m
10. ein Kartenspiel n
11. eine Fahne
12. Fanschminke f

1. una taza firmada
2. un reloj deportivo
3. una banderola/ banderín
4. un estuche
5. un paraguas
6. una regla
7. un disco compacto
8. una chapa
9. una mini camiseta para el coche
10. una baraja de cartas
11. una bandera
12. el maquillaje de los aficionados

ADDITIONAL LANGUAGE:

1. un portefeuille
2. un porte-monnaie
3. un autocollant
4. un écusson
5. un trophée
6. une carte postale (d'un) joueur
7. une photo (d'un) joueur
8. un coussin (pour siège du stade)
9. une crécelle
10. un sac banane
11. un livre d'autographes

1. wallet
2. purse
3. sticker
4. badge
5. trophy
6. postcard - player
7. photo - player
8. cushion (for stadium seat)
9. football rattle
10. bum bag
11. autograph book

SUGGESTED ACTIVITIES:

- Selected activities from Unit 2.
- DIY Matching Pairs - Souvenirs and Prices

More Souvenirs

© MiniFlashcards

14 Shopping Role Play

SUGGESTED LANGUAGE:

A Good morning.
B Good morning.
A Can I help you?
B Yes, a flag, please.
A Large or small?
B Large, please.
A Here you are.
   Anything else?
B A shirt, please.
A Long or short
   sleeves?
B Short, please.
A Here you are.
B How much is that?
A X pounds/pence.
B Here you are.
A Thank you.
   Goodbye.
B Thank you.
   Goodbye

A Bonjour.
B Bonjour.
A Vous désirez?
B Un drapeau, svp.
A Grand ou petit?
B Un grand, svp.
A Voilà. Et autre
   chose?
B Un maillot.
A A manches
   longues ou courtes?
B Courtes, svp.
A Voilà.
B Ça fait combien?
A X francs.
B Voilà.
A Merci, et au revoir.
B Merci. Au revoir.

A Guten Tag.
B Guten Tag.
A Was möchtest du?
B Eine Fahne, bitte.
A Groß oder klein/
   Eine große oder
   kleine?
B Eine große, bitte.
A Hier bitte. Sonst
   noch etwas?
B Ein Trikot/Hemd,
   bitte.
A Mit langen oder
   kurzen Ärmeln?
B Mit kurzen, bitte.
A Bitte sehr.
B Was macht das?
A X Mark/Pfennig.
B Bitte.
A Danke und auf
   Wiedersehn.
B Danke, tschüs.

A Buenos días.
B Buenos dias.
A ¿Qué desea?
B Una bandera,
   por favor.
A ¿Grande o
   pequeña?
B Grande, por favor.
A Aquí tiene. ¿Algo
   más?
B Una camisa, por
   favor.
A ¿De manga larga o
   manga corta?
B De manga corta,
   por favor.
A Aquí tiene.
B ¿Cuánto cuesta?
A X pesetas.
B Aquí tiene.
A Gracias. ¡Adiós!
B Gracias. ¡Adiós!

SUGGESTED ACTIVITY:

- Cut the picture Role Play into two Sections A and B. Two learners act out the roles of A, the souvenir shop assistant, and B, the fan. A third learner can be provided with a sample dialogue as above, and act as observer/prompter.
- Use as a model for additional roleplays.

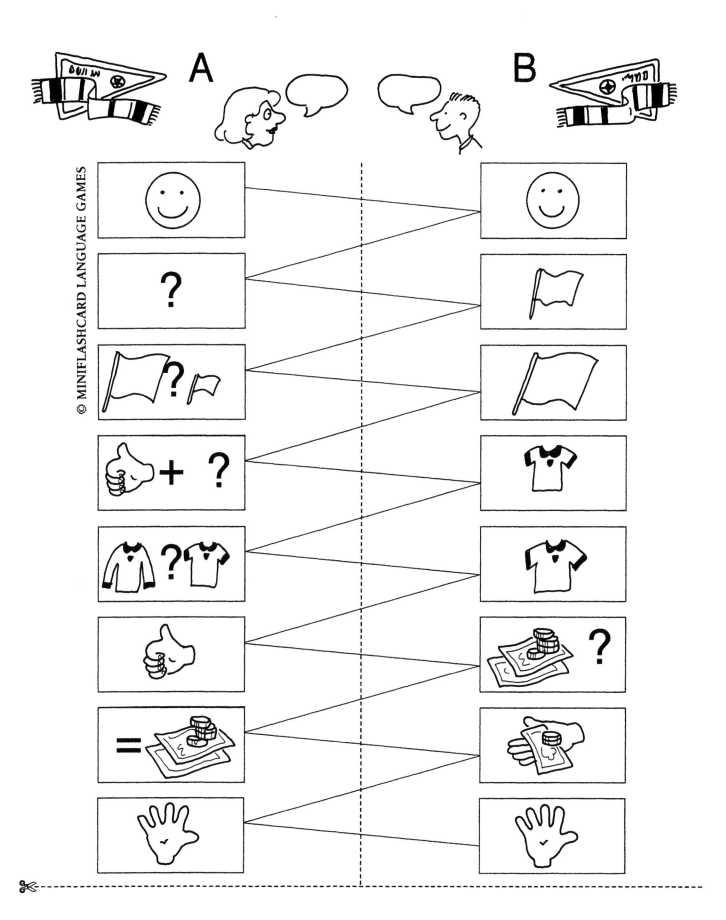

© MINIFLASHCARD LANGUAGE GAMES

15   Football Kit

La tenue de foot

SUGGESTED LANGUAGE:

1. short sleeved shirt/top	1. un maillot à manches courtes	1. kurzärmeliges Hemd	1. una camisa de manga corta
2. long sleeved shirt/top	2. un maillot à manches longues	2. langärmeliges Hemd	2. una camisa de manga larga
3. shorts	3. un short	3. Shorts/Hose	3. los pantalones cortos
4. cycling shorts	4. un cuissard/un short de cycliste	4. Radlerhosen pl	4. los pantalones de ciclista
5. socks	5. des chaussettes f (de foot)	5. Sportsocken pl	5. los calcetines
6. football boots	6. des chaussures f de foot	6. Fußballschuhe/-stiefel pl	6. las botas de fútbol
7. laces	7. les lacets m	7. Schnürsenkel pl	7. los cordones
8. shinguards	8. des protège-tibias m	8. Schienbeinschützer pl	8. las espinilleras
9. gloves	9. des gants m	9. Handschuhe pl	9. los guantes
10. support bandage	10. un bandage élastique	10. Stützverband m	10. una venda elástica
11. home/away strip	11. la tenue de match à domicile/ à l'extérieur	11. Dreß für Auswärtsspiele m	11. el traje de los partidos en casa / de los partidos fuera
12. tracksuit	12. un survêtement	12. ein Trainingsanzug m	12. un chándal

ADDITIONAL LANGUAGE:

1. confortable	1. comfortable
2. durable	2. durable
3. léger	3. lightweight
4. cher	4. expensive
5. bon marché	5. cheap
6. en coton	6. made of cotton
7. en matériel synthétique	7. made of synthetic material
8. en cuir	8. made of leather
9. propre	9. clean
10. sale	10. dirty
11. couvert de boue	11. muddy
12. laver	12. to wash
13. repasser	13. to iron

SUGGESTED ACTIVITIES:
- Selected activities from Unit 2.
- DIY Matching Pairs - items and price tickets.
- Survey - classmates' views on:
  Le nombre d'équipements - Number of kits per team.
  Le coût des équipements, des affaires de foot - Cost of kits.
- Describe how you take care of your kit.
- Link to Unit 50 - Souvenir Order Form.

Football Kit

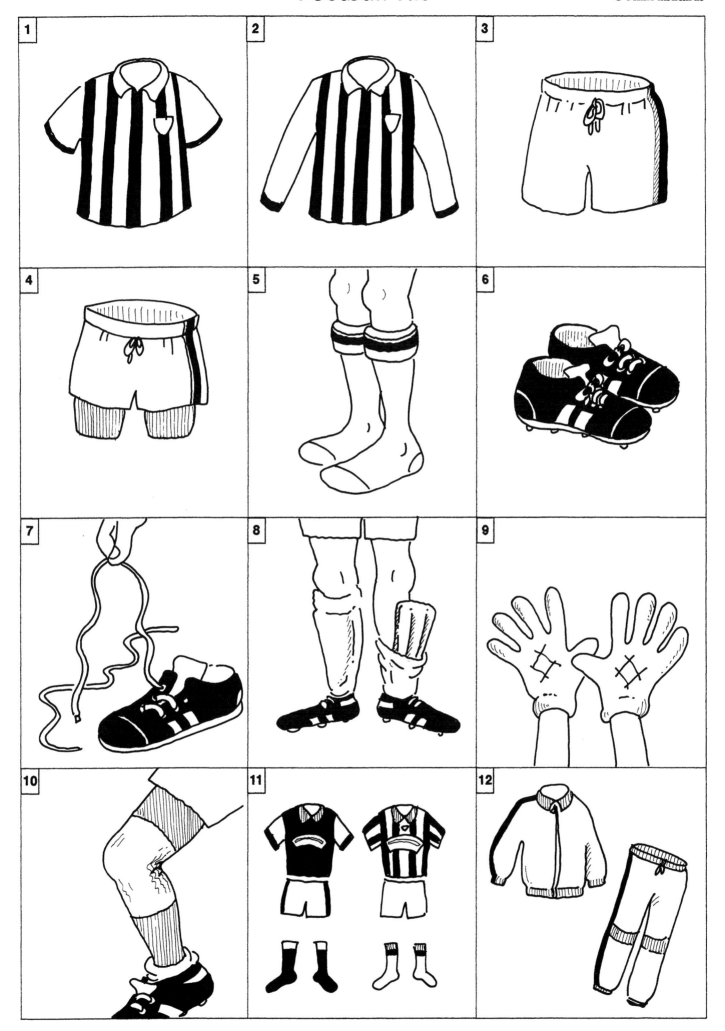

16 Colours of Kit - Tick Grid

SUGGESTED LANGUAGE:

See previous sheet, plus colours.

SUGGESTED ACTIVITIES:

- Colour in the blobs in a range of colours to match those of popular football strips.
- Choose colour combinations for your kit, then read them out to the rest of the group who fill in their grids.
- Play 'Guess the Kit colours' then compare with a kit chosen by another.
- Make up other combinations of clothes and equipment, using the template.

Tick Grid - Colours of Kit

	◯	◯	◯	◯	◯	◯

17   Other Clothes and Accessories

SUGGESTED LANGUAGE:

1. cap	1. une casquette	1. eine Schirmmütze	1. una gorra
2. Bronx hat	2. un bonnet	2. eine (Strick/Woll)Mütze	2. un gorro
3. scarf	3. une écharpe		3. una bufanda
4. trainers	4. des baskets m	3. ein Schal	4. las zapatillas de deporte
5. sweatshirt	5. un sweat	4. Turnschuhe pl	
6. T-shirt	6. un T-shirt	5. ein Sweatshirt	5. una sudadera
7. shirt	7. un chemisier/une chemise	6. ein T-shirt	6. una camiseta
8. tie with shield		7. ein Hemd	7. una camisa
9. blazer	8. une cravate blason	8. ein Schlips mit Emblem/Trophäe	8. una corbata con escudo
10. trousers	9. un blazer		
11. sports bag	10. un pantalon	9. ein Blazer	9. una americana
12. rucksack	11. un sac de sport	10. eine Hose	10. los pantalones
	12. un sac à dos	11. eine Sporttasche	11. una bolsa de deportes
		12. ein Rucksack	12. una mochila

SUGGESTED ACTIVITIES:

- Selected activities from Unit 2.
- DIY Matching Pairs - items and price tickets.
- Link to Unit 50 - Souvenir Order Form.

More Clothes

© MiniFlashcards

18 Football Kit - Beetle

SUGGESTED LANGUAGE:

1. a cap	1. une casquette	1. eine Schirmmütze	1. una gorra
2. a shirt	2. un maillot	2. ein Trikot/Hemd	2. una camisa/ camiseta
3. a pair of shorts	3. un short	3. ein Paar Shorts/ eine Hose	3. un calzón corto
4. a glove	4. un gant	4. ein Handschuh m	4. un guante
5. a sock	5. une chaussette	5. ein Stutzen m	5. un calcetín
6. a shoe	6. une chaussure	6. ein Schuh m	6. una bota

SUGGESTED ACTIVITIES:

Photocopy a number of Football Kit pictures and cut into sections. Learners can draw in stripes etc and colour them in.

Beetle   (One set of cards per player. 6 sided dice)

Spread the cards out over the table. Throw the dice and ask for an item of kit that matches the dice number. The first player to complete their kit wins.

Variation: Cut out pictures of players from magazines, cut them up and paste onto card. Players collect parts of the same or different players.

Variation: **Rummy**   (One set of cards per player plus an extra set)
Deal out 12 cards each and put the rest in the centre of the table. Ask the player on your left for a card eg *une casquette svp.* If s/he does not have the piece of kit you need, you pick up a card from the pile. If you can use it, you keep it and discard one. The first player to collect a complete kit wins.

Variation: **Happy Families**
As for Rummy but collect sets of items of kit eg *caps* or *gloves*.

Football Kit - Beetle

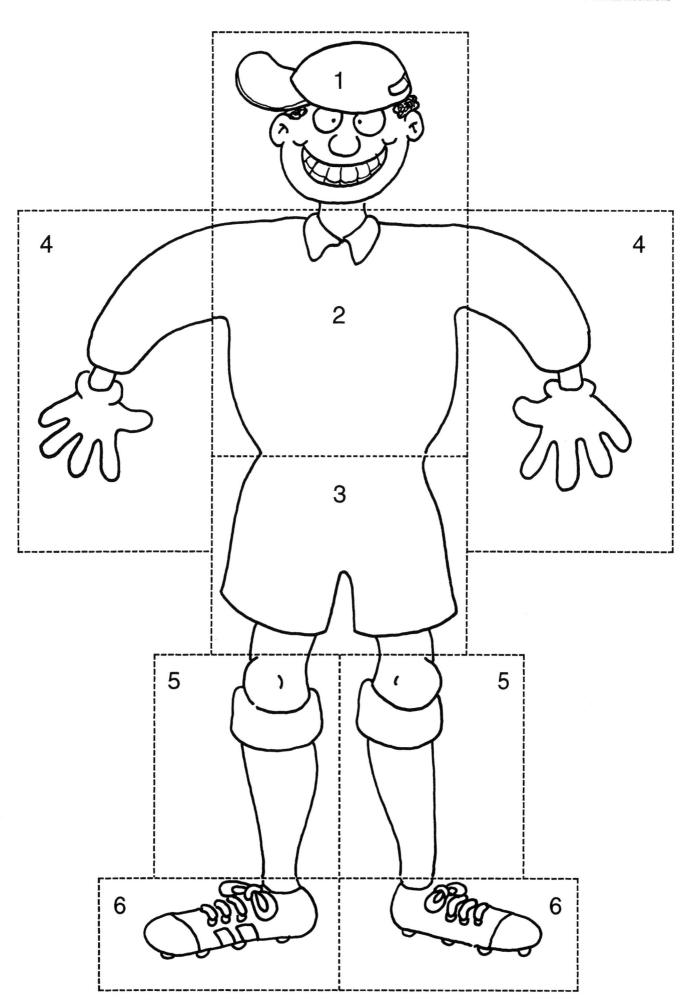

19　Some Fans

Des fans

Some pictures of fans - what they look like and what they are wearing.

SUGGESTED LANGUAGE:

1. *un jeune homme de 20 ans, aux cheveux blonds et courts, au visage peint*
   portant un jean, un blouson et un T-shirt à rayures.
2. *une fille de 17 ans, aux cheveux longs et noirs,*
   portant un maillot et un short.
3. *un homme de 70 ans, moustache et lunettes,*
   portant un manteau, une écharpe à rayures et un chapeau.
4. *un garcon de 10 ans, aux cheveux courts,*
   portant un jean, un blouson, une écharpe, et un chapeau.
5. *un jeune homme de 18 ans, aux cheveux très courts - un 'skinhead,'*
   portant un jean, un T-shirt à rayures et des bottes.
6. *un homme de 55 ans, aux cheveux noirs, barbu,*
   portant des lunettes
   portant un imperméable avec un coussin et un thermos.
7. *une femme de 40 ans, aux cheveux châtains*
   portant un manteau, une écharpe, un chapeau et un sac.
8. *une femme de 60 ans, aux cheveux gris et portant des lunettes,*
   portant une jupe, une veste, des bottes et un bonnet
9. *un jeune homme de 20 ans,*
   portant un sweat, un jean et une écharpe.

1. *a young man about 20, with short blond hair, and face paint*
   wearing jeans, a jacket and a striped T-shirt.
2. *a girl about 17, with long black hair*
   wearing a striped shirt and shorts.
3. *a man about 70, with a moustache and glasses*
   wearing an overcoat, a striped scarf and a hat.
4. *a boy about 10, with short hair*
   wearing jeans, a jacket, scarf and hat.
5. *a skinhead around 18*
   wearing jeans, a striped T shirt and boots.
6. *a man around 55, with black hair, a beard and glasses*
   wearing a raincoat and carrying a cushion and flask.
7. *a woman around 40, with dark hair*
   wearing a coat, a scarf and a hat, and with a bag
8. *a woman around 60 with grey hair and glasses*
   wearing a skirt, a jacket, boots and a woolly hat.
9. *a youth around 20*
   wearing a sweatshirt, jeans, a scarf and a Bronx hat.

ADDITIONAL LANGUAGE:

Qu'est-ce que je vais mettre/porter?
Je vais porter un jean, un blouson et un T-shirt à rayures, et aussi ma casquette et mes lunettes de soleil.
Je vais me peindre le visage aux couleurs de mon équipe.

What shall I put on/wear?
I'll wear jeans, a jacket, and a striped T shirt and also my cap and my sun glasses.
I'm going to paint my face in my team colours.

SUGGESTED ACTIVITIES:

- Selected games from Unit 2.
- Practise tenses.
- Imagine which team they support, and whether their team won or lost. Match to mood cards in Unit 49.

- Who went to a match last Saturday? What did you wear?
- Who is going to the match next Saturday? What are you going to wear?
- Cut out some magazine pictures, or video a match and look at a still. Describe some fans.
- Link weather/clothes.

Fans

© MiniFlashcards

20 Verbs - Fans

Les activités des fans

SUGGESTED LANGUAGE:

1. *lire*
2. *manger*
3. *boire*
4. *applaudir*
5. *crier*
6. *siffler*
7. *chanter/scander*
8. *pleurer*
9. *s'étreindre/se féliciter*
10. *sauter de joie*
11. *agiter (des drapeaux, des mascottes)*
12. *battre du tambour*

1. *read*
2. *eat*
3. *drink*
4. *clap*
5. *shout*
6. *whistle*
7. *sing/chant*
8. *cry*
9. *hug*
10. *leap for joy*
11. *wave (flags, mascots)*
12. *beat drums*

1. *lesen*
2. *essen*
3. *trinken*
4. *klatschen/ applaudieren*
5. *schreien*
6. *pfeifen*
7. *singen*
8. *weinen*
9. *umarmen*
10. *vor Freude in die Luft springen*
11. *schwingen (eine Fahne, ein Maskottchen)*
12. *trommeln*

1. *leer*
2. *comer*
3. *beber*
4. *aplaudir*
5. *gritar*
6. *silbar*
7. *cantar/corear*
8. *llorar*
9. *abrazar*
10. *saltar de alegría*
11. *ondear (banderas, mascotas)*
12. *tocar los tambores*

SUGGESTED ACTIVITIES:

- Selected activities from Unit 2.
- Charades.

Verbs - Fans

© MiniFlashcards

21   Some of the People

Les métiers du foot

Some of the people involved. Not just the players, but support staff also.

SUGGESTED LANGUAGE:

1. mascot	1. la mascotte	1. das Maskottchen	1. la mascota
2. captain	2. le capitaine	2. der Kapitän	2. el capitán
3. player	3. le joueur / la joueuse	3. der Spieler/ die Spielerin	3. el jugador
4. (goal)keeper	4. le gardien de but	4. der Torwart	4. el portero
5. referee	5. l'arbitre mf	5. der Schiedsrichter	5. el árbitro
6. assistant referee	6. juge (mf) de touche	6. der Lienienrichter	6. el juez del línea
7. substitute	7. remplaçant(e) m(f)	7. der Auswechselspieler	7. el suplente
8. physiotherapist	8. kinésithérapeute mf	8. der Physiotherapeut	8. el/la fisioterapeuta
9. coach	9. l'entraîneur / l'entraîneuse	9. der Trainer	9. el entrenador
10. manager	10. le directeur/ le manager	10. der Manager	10. el representante
11. commentator	11. le commentateur	11. der Reporter	11. el comentarista
12. photographer	12. photographe mf	12. der Fotograf	12. el fotógrafo

ADDITIONAL LANGUAGE

1. l'équipe f /le groupe	1. squad
2. l'équipe f	2. team
3. le ramasseur/la ramasseuse de balles	3. ballgirl/boy, ballkid
4. le porteur/la porteuse de drapeau	4. flag carrier
5. le vigile	5. security guard
6. le sponsor	6. sponsor
7. le président	7. chairman
8. le policier	8. police officer
9. le pompier	9. fire officer
10. le médecin	10. doctor

SUGGESTED ACTIVITIES:

- Selected games from Unit 2.

- DIY Matching Pairs: What do the different people do? What do they wear? How much do you think they earn?
- Which one would you like to be? Why?
- Quiz - Name some well known people - what are they ? (player for X club, for X position, manager etc)
- Describe *A Day in the Life of...*

Some of the People

© MiniFlashcards

22 Verbs - Players

Les activités des joueurs

Non-technical verbs.

SUGGESTED LANGUAGE:

1. stand/watch	1. se tenir (debout)/ observer	1. stehen/ beobachten	1. estar de pie/ver
2. shake hands	2. se serrer la main	2. Hände schütteln	2. dar la mano
3. run	3. courir	3. laufen/rennen	3. correr
4. jump	4. sauter	4. springen	4. saltar
5. throw	5. lancer	5. werfen	5. tirar
6. kick	6. donner un coup de pied dans le ballon/tirer	6. kicken/treten	6. dar una patada, patear
7. dive	7. plonger	7. tauchen	7. lanzarse
8. hug	8. s'étreindre/se féliciter	8. umarmen	8. abrazar
9. push	9. pousser	9. schubsen	9. empujar
10. trip someone up	10. faire un croche-pied à quelqu'un	10. jemandem ein Bein stellen	10. hacer una zancadilla a alguien
11. lie on the ground	11. être étendu par terre	11. auf dem Boden liegen	11. tumbarse en el campo
12. argue (with the ref)	12. se disputer/discuter avec l'arbitre	12. streiten (mit dem Schiedsrichter)	12. discutir/ (con el arbitro)

ADDITIONAL LANGUAGE:

1. le gardien de but a plongé pour bloquer le ballon
2. il a lancé le ballon à 50 mètres
3. il est étendu par terre
4. les joueurs s'embrassent et se congratulent après un but
5. le joueur mécontent discute avec l'arbitre

1. the keeper dived for the ball
2. he threw the ball 50 metres
3. he's lying on the ground
4. the players hug each other after a goal
5. the angry player is arguing with the ref

SUGGESTED ACTIVITIES:

- Selected activities from Unit 2.
- Cut out the pictures. Listen to a sequence of events given by another and put the cards in the correct order.

Verbs - Players

© MiniFlashcards

23   Dream Team

Mon équipe de rêve

1. a (goal)keeper	1. un gardien de but	1. ein Torwart	1. un portero
2. defenders	2. des défenseurs	2. Verteidiger	2. los defensas
3. midfield players	3. des milieux de terrain	3. Mittelfeldspieler	3. los centrocampistas
4. forwards/attackers	4. des attaquants	4. Angriffsspieler/ Stürmer	4. los delanteros
5. winger	5. un ailier	5. Linksaussen/ Rechtsaussen	5. un extremo
6. striker	6. un avant centre	6. der Stürmer	6. un ariete
7. sweeper	7. un arrière volant/libéro	7. der Libero	7. un líbero
8. centre back	8. un arrière centre	8. der Vorstopper	8. un defensa central
9. opponent	9. un adversaire	9. ein Gegner	9. un oponente

ADDITIONAL LANGUAGE:

1. right-footed	1. droitier
2. left-footed	2. gaucher
3. attackers have to get goals	3. les attaquants sont chargés de marquer les buts
4. defenders and keepers must stop goals	4. les défenseurs et le gardien de but doivent arrêter les buts
5. midfielders have to be both attacker and defender	5. les milieux de terrain doivent être à la fois défenseurs et attaquants
6. nowadays each player's game is becoming more versatile	6. actuellement le jeu de chaque joueur devient plus polyvalent
7. total football	7. le football total
8. Some popular formations: the 5.3.2, the 4.4.2, the 4.3.3, the 3.5.3, the 5.2.3	8. Des systèmes populaires: le 5.3.2, le 4.4.2, le 4.3.3, le 3.5.3, le 5.2.3
9. what's the system of your favourite team?	9. quel est le système de ton équipe favorite?
:	

SUGGESTED ACTIVITIES:

- Pick one of the formations and draw up your Dream Team, filling in names and positions on the chart. Add a short description of each player. See Units 4 and 51 - My Favourite Player.
  Il s'appelle...
- Cut and paste components of the chart to make your own favourite formation.
- Selected activities from Unit 2 eg DIY Matching Pairs, True or False, Bingo, I Went to Market..., Battleship Buddies, Kim's game - (Who's been sent off ?- Player number X from Toulouse.)
- Make up and play a Dream Team version of Beetle with a 12 sided spinner or two 6 sided dice. Collect the 11 players in your team (name the players and positions) plus a substitute or the coach.
- Make up quizzes on: - well known players - what positions they play.
  - well known teams - what systems they use.
- Number the players and use to practise prepositions.

Dream Team 1

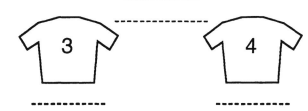

Dream Team 2

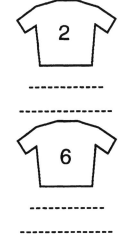
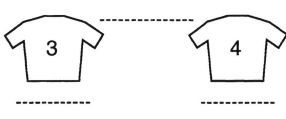

24   Body - Injuries

Blessures

SUGGESTED LANGUAGE:

1. s/he's hurt his/her head	1. il/elle s'est fait mal à la tête	1. er/sie hat sich am Kopf verletzt	El/Ella se ha lastimado...
2. he's hurt his nose	2. il s'est fait mal au nez	2. er hat sich der Nase verletzt	
3. he's hurt his teeth	3. il s'est fait mal aux dents f	3. er hat sich die Zähne verletzt	1. la cebeza
4. he's hurt his hand	4. il s'est fait mal à la main	4. er hat sich an der Hand verletzt	2. la nariz
5. he's hurt his shoulder	5. il s'est fait mal à l'épaule f	5. er hat sich an der Schulter verletzt	3. los dientes
6. he's hurt his leg	6. il s'est fait mal à la jambe	6. er hat sich am Bein verletzt	4. la mano
7. he's hurt his toe	7. il s'est fait mal à l'orteil m	7. er hat sich am Zeh verletzt	5. el hombro
8. he's hurt his neck	8. il s'est fait mal au cou	8. er hat sich am Hals verletzt	6. la pierna
9. he's hurt his back	9. il s'est fait mal au dos	9. er hat sich am Rücken verletzt	7. un dedo del pie
10. he's hurt his finger	10. il s'est fait mal au doigt	10. er hat sich am Finger verletzt	8. el cuello
11. he's hurt his knee/the trainer's on the field	11. il s'est fait mal au genou/l'entraîneur est sur le terrain	11. er hat sich am Knie verletzt/ der Trainer ist auf dem Spielfeld	9. la espalda
12. he's going off on a stretcher	12. il quitte le terrain sur un brancard	12. er wird auf einer Trage weggetragen	10. un dedo
			11. se ha lastimado la rodilla/ el entrenador está en el campo
			12. se va en una camilla

ADDITIONAL LANGUAGE:

1. se blesser	1. to injure
2. il/elle se blesse au pied	2. s/he injures his/her foot
3. l'oeil m	3. eye
4. l'oreille f	4. ear
5. le bras	5. arm
6. le pied	6. foot
7. il saigne du nez	7. he's got a nosebleed
8. il s'est cassé la jambe	8. he's broken his leg
9. il s'est foulé la cheville	9. he's sprained his ankle
10. il s'est déchiré un muscle	10. he's pulled a muscle
11. il s'est froissé un ligament	11. he's strained a ligament
12. il s'est froissé un muscle dans l'aine f	12. he's got groin strain
13. le tendon du jarret	13. hamstring
14. le tendon d'Achille	14. Achilles' tendon
15. le mollet	15. calf
16. il a une commotion cérébrale	16. he's got concussion
17. il a soif	17. he's thirsty
18. il est déshydraté	18. he's dehydrated

SUGGESTED ACTIVITIES:

- Selected activities from Unit 2 eg Charades.
- Convert to present tense as in football commentaries eg *Just before half-time, X injures his back.*
- Convert a football commentary (present) to newspaper report (past).
- Imagine a conversation between an injured player and a physio on the pitch.

Body - Injuries

25   The Magic First Aid Kit!

La trousse de premier secours

SUGGESTED LANGUAGE:

1. plaster
2. bandage
3. elastic support bandage
4. compress
5. cream
6. tablet/pain killer
7. bottle of massage oil
8. the famous analgesic spray
9. ice
10. cold water
11. sponge
12. stretcher

1. un pansement
2. un bandage
3. un bandage élastique
4. une compresse
5. de la crème
6. un comprimé contre la douleur
7. un flacon d'huile de massage
8. la fameuse 'bombe à froid' pour soulager les douleurs
9. de la glace
10. de l'eau froide
11. une éponge
12. un brancard

1. ein Pflaster m
2. ein Verband m
3. ein elastischer Stützverband
4. eine Kompresse
5. ein Salbe/Creme
6. eine Tablette/ Schmerztablette
7. eine Flasche Massageöl
8. das berühmte schmerzstillende Spray/Eisspray
9. Eis n
10. kaltes Wasser
11. der Schwamm
12. die Trage/ Tragbahre

1. una tirita
2. vendas
3. un vendaje elástico
4. una compresa
5. crema
6. un comprimido contra el dolor
7. un bote de aceite para masaje
8. el famoso espray analgésico
9. hielo m
10. agua fría f
11. una esponja
12. una camilla

ADDITIONAL LANGUAGE:

1. un rouleau de sparadrap
2. du (produit) désinfectant
3. une attelle
4. une boisson
5. une serviette
6. on l'a sorti du terrain sur un brancard
7. il recevait des soins hors du terrain

1. roll of sticking plaster
2. disinfectant
3. splint
4. drink
5. towel
6. he was carried off the field on a stretcher
7. he was off the field having treatment

SUGGESTED ACTIVITIES:

- Selected activities from Unit 2 eg Charades, I Went to Market, Beat the Clock.
- Matching Pairs - Match Injuries and First Aid Treatment.

The Magic First Aid Kit!

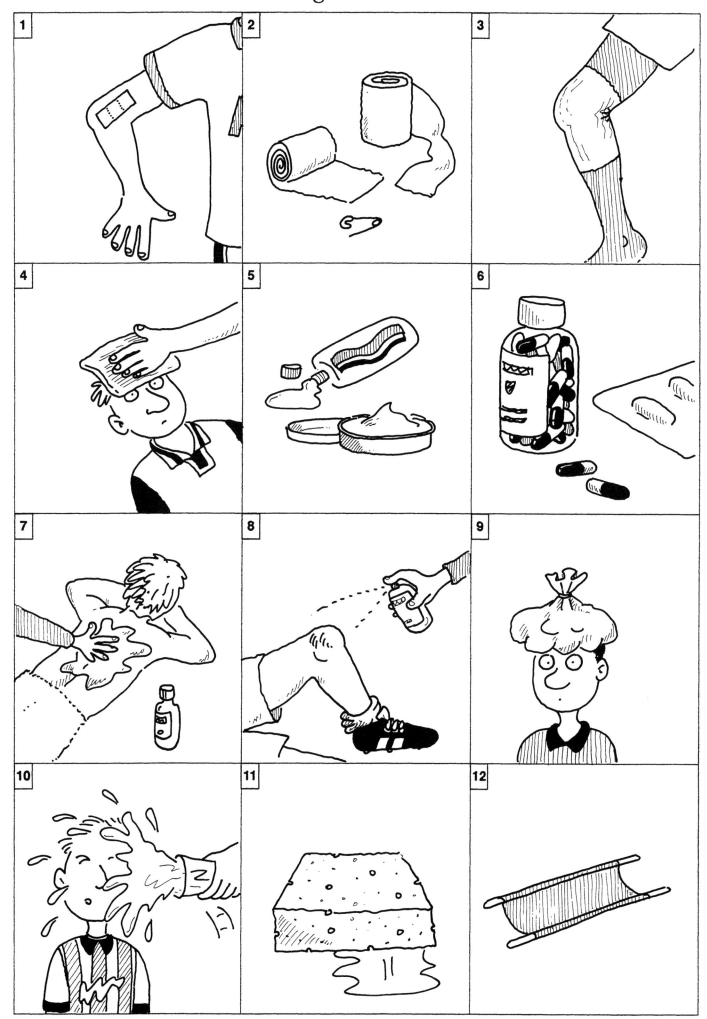

26 Football Table - Information Gap

Les résultats

SUGGESTED LANGUAGE:

1. results	1. résultats	1. Ergebnisse	1. resultados
2. points	2. point*	2. Punkte	2. puntos
3. matches played	3. match joué*	3. Spiele gespielt	3. partidos jugados
4. matches won	4. match gagné*	4. Spiele gewonnen	4. partidos ganados
5. matches drawn	5. match nul*	5. Spiele unentschieden gespielt	5. partidos empatados
6. matches lost	6. match perdu*	6. Spiele verloren	6. partidos perdidos
7. goals scored	7. but marqué*	7. Tore	7. goles marcados
8. goals conceded	8. but encaissé*	8. Gegentore	8. goles concedidos

SUGGESTED ACTIVITIES:

- Cut each set of results into 2. In pairs, ask each other questions to fill in the gaps.
- Use also as a dictation exercise.
- *Variation:* Learners make up (word process) a blank football match results sheet, ready to fill in the score. Use as a dictation exercise for the week's football match results. To make it more difficult, read out the results in a different order from that on the sheet (as though the results are in the process of coming in).

*(NB In French magazines these headings
appear in the singular)

RÉSULTATS

Résultats du Mois – Angleterre – 25e Journée

	Point	Match Joué	Match Gagné	Match Nul	Match Perdu	But Marqué	But Encaissé
	50		15	5			19
Chelsea		25				52	
	45	25	13		6		
Crystal Palace		24			11	21	34
Bolton		25		11		22	41
Barnsley	22	25	6	4	15	22	
Manchester		25			5	52	
	45		14	3	8		27
Liverpool		25		6		41	22
	23	24	5	8			
	23	25	4		10	22	
Barnsley		25	6				61

Résultats du Mois – France – 25e Journée

	Point	Match Joué	Match Gagné	Match Nul	Match Perdu	But Marqué	But Encaissé
Marseille			14		6		17
	47	25		8		36	
Monaco		25	14				23
	23	25			12		37
		25	6	5	14	23	
Cannes	22	25	6	4			44
	47	25		5		35	
Metz		25	13		4		20
	46	25		4	7	39	
Strasbourg		25	5	8		28	
Châteauroux	23						47
		25			15	25	

27 Prepositions - Spot the Ball!

Où est le ballon?

SUGGESTED LANGUAGE:

Le ballon est/the ball is:

1. in the drawer	1. dans le tiroir	1. in der Schublade	1. en el cajón
2. on his head	2. sur sa tête	2. auf seinem Kopf	2. sobre su cabeza
3. behind the computer	3. derrière l'ordinateur	3. hinter dem Computer	3. detrás del ordenador
4. in the bin	4. dans la corbeille	4. im Papierkorb	4. en la papelera
5. on the shelf	5. sur le rayon /l'étagère f	5. auf dem Regal	5. en el estante
6. in the cupboard	6. dans le placard	6. im Schrank	6. en el armario
7. under the table	7. sous la table	7. unter dem Tisch	7. debajo de la mesa
8. in front of the bin	8. devant la corbeille	8. vor dem Papierkorb	8. delante de la papelera
9. between the tables	9. entre les tables	9. zwischen den Tischen	9. entre las mesas
10. behind the door	10. derrière la porte	10. hinter der Tür	10. detrás de la puerta
11. under the chair	11. sous la chaise	11. unter dem Stuhl	11. debajo de la silla
12. on his foot	12. sur son pied	12. auf seinem Fuß	12. en su pie

SUGGESTED ACTIVITIES:

- Selected activities from Unit 2.
- The teacher puts a football in a different place in the classroom each lesson - sometimes visible, sometimes hidden - pupils have to say or guess where it is.

Prepositions - Spot the Ball

Les photos des équipes

Spot the Differences between the players in the local game and in the big media event!

SUGGESTED LANGUAGE:

1. on	1. sur	1. auf	1. en
2. under	2. sous	2. unter	2. debajo de
3. next to	3. à côté de	3. neben	3. al lado de
4. behind	4. derrière	4. hinter	4. detrás de
5. in front of	5. devant	5. vor	5. delante de
6. between	6. entre	6. zwischen	6. entre
7. in the front row	7. au premier rang	7. in der ersten Reihe (vorne)	7. en primera línea
8. in the back row	8. au fond	8. in der letzten Reihe (hinten)	8. al fondo
9. on the right	9. à droite	9. rechts	9. a la derecha
10. on the left	10. à gauche	10. links	10. a la izquierda
11. in the middle	11. au milieu	11. in der Mitte	11. en el medio

SUGGESTED ACTIVITIES:

- Number the players in Picture A and use to play Spot the Difference with Picture B.
- Selected activities from Unit 2 eg True or False, Guessing Game.
- Use to practise prepositions.
- Use also to describe:
  What players look like, of various ages/fitness levels.
  The various styles of kit.
  What team members might be thinking or saying to each other.

Prepositions - Photocall

Guide Télé

SUGGESTED LANGUAGE:

Impossible d'obtenir des billets pour le match? Ne désespérez pas! Restez à la maison avec une pizza et des copains et partagez vos impressions!

Etablissez votre Guide Télé de Foot pour la semaine!

Semaine commençant:

Lundi
Mardi
Mercredi
Jeudi
Vendredi
Samedi
Dimanche

La Chaîne:
L'heure:
Présenté par:
Invités:
Commentaires de:
Un programme consacré à:

Impossible to get tickets for the big match? All is not lost! Stay at home with a pizza and some friends and share your reactions!

Draw up your football viewing schedule for the week!

Week beginning:

Monday
Tuesday
Wednesday
Thursday
Friday
Saturday
Sunday

Channel:
Time:
Presented by:
Guests:
Commentary by:
A programme featuring/about:

Unmöglich, Karten für das Spitzenspiel zu bekommen? Noch ist nicht alles verloren. Bleibt zu Hause mit einer Pizza und ein paar Freunden und teilt eure Reaktionen!

Plant euer Fernsehen für die ganze Woche!

Woche ab:

Montag
Dienstag
Mittwoch
Donnerstag
Freitag
Samstag
Sonntag

Programm/Sender:
Zeit:
Präsentiert von/Moderiert bei:
Gäste:
Kommentiert von:
Ein Programm über:

¿Es imposible conseguir entradas para el gran partido? No está todo perdido. Quédate en casa con una pizza y algunos amigos y compartid vuestras reacciones.

¡Establece tu programa de fútbol para la semana!

Comienzo de la semana:

Lunes
Martes
Miércoles
Jueves
Viernes
Sábado
Domingo

El canal:
La hora:
Presentado por:
Invitados:
Comentado por:
Un programa sobre:

30 Surveys

Sondages

SUGGESTED LANGUAGE:

Tu aimes le foot? Oui/non
Pourquoi/pas?

Do you like football? Yes/No.
Why?/Why not?

Tu regardes le foot à la télé?
Quand?
Tu regardes la télé satellite?
Quand?
Tu écoutes la radio?
Quand?

Do you watch football on TV?
When?
Do you watch satellite TV?
When?
Do you listen to the radio?
When?

Tu es supporter de quelle équipe?
Tu vas aux matchs?
Quand?
Qu'est-ce que tu portes?
Comment tu y vas?
Qu'est-ce que tu manges/bois?

What team do you support?
Do you go to the matches?
When?
What do you wear?
How do you get there?
What do you eat/drink?

Quel est ton joueur favori?
Quel/qui est le meilleur
joueur/gardien/capitaine/entraîneur/manager?
Quel/qui est le pire/plus mauvais?

Who's your favourite player?
Who is the best player/goalkeeper/captain/coach
/manager?
Who's the worst?

Quel/qui est le plus beau joueur?
Qui a la meilleure coupe de cheveux/coiffure?
Qui a la plus mauvaise coupe?
Que penses-tu des cheveux de X?

Who's the best looking player?
Who's got the best haircut?
Who's got the worst haircut?
What do you think of X's hair?

Que penses tu....?

What do you think....?

Quels joueurs vont être sélectionnés?
Est-ce que X va jouer?
Est-ce que X va être en forme pour jouer?
Qui va être sur le banc?
Qui va être capitaine?
X va jouer quelle position?
Qui va jouer avant centre? (etc)
Qui va marquer un but?
Qui va gagner le match?
Quel va être le score?
Qui va recevoir un carton jaune/rouge?
Qui va être le joueur du match?
Qui va gagner la Coupe?
Quelle équipe va descendre (au classement)?
Quelle équipe va monter au classement?

Which players are going to be selected?
Is X going to be playing?
Is X going to be fit to play?
Who's going to be on the bench?
Who's going to be captain?
What position is X going to play in?
Who's going to play eg centre forward?
Who's going to get a goal?
Who's going to win the game?
What's the score going to be?
Who's going to get a yellow/red card?
Who's going to be player of the match?
Who's going to win the cup?
Which team's going to go down/be relegated?
Which team's going to go up/be promoted?

SUGGESTED ACTIVITIES:

Carry out a survey amongst your classmates or other people. Present the information in chart form for the Coin Football. Make awards to those who have made accurate predictions!

Magst du Fußball? Ja/nein
Warum/warum nicht?

Guckst du Fußball im Fernsehen?
Wann?
Guckst du Satellitenfernsehen?
Wann?
Hörst du Radio?
Wann?

Du bist Fan von welcher Mannschaft?
Gehst du zu den Spielen?
Wann?
Was trägst du/ziehst du an?
Wie kommst du dort hin?
Was ißt/trinkst du?

Wer ist dein Lieblingsspieler?
Wer ist der beste...
Spieler/Torwart/Kapitän/Trainer/Manager?
Wer ist der schlechteste?

Welcher Spieler sieht am besten aus?
Wer hat den besten Haarschnitt?
Wer hat den schlechtesten Haarschnitt?
Was hälst du von Xs Haar?

Was meinst du/hälst du von...?

Welche Spieler werden ausgewählt?
Wird X spielen?
Wird X fit sein?
Wer wird auf der Bank sitzen?
Wer wird der Kapitän?
Auf welcher Position wird X spielen?
Wer wird z.B. Mittelstürmer spielen?
Wer erzielt/schießt ein Tor?
Wer gewinnt das Spiel?
Wie wird das Spiel ausgehen?
Wer bekommt eine gelbe/rote Karte?
Wer wird Spieler des Tages?
Wer gewinnt den Pokal?
Welche Mannschaft steigt ab?
Welche Mannschaft steigt auf?

¿Te gusta el fútbol? Si/no.
¿Por qué? ¿Por qué no?

¿Ves fútbol por la tele?
¿Cuándo?
¿Ves la televisión vía satelíte?
¿Cuándo?
¿Escuchas la radio?
¿Cuándo?

¿De qué equipo eres?
¿Vas a los partidos?
¿Cuándo?
¿Qué llevas puesto?
¿Cómo vas?
¿Qué bebes/comes?

¿Quién es tu jugador favorito?
¿Quién es el mejor...
jugador/portero/capitán/entrenador/representante?
¿Quién es el peor?

¿Quién es el jugador más guapo?
¿Quién lleva el mejor corte de pelo?
¿Quién lleva el peor corte de pelo?
¿Qué piensas del pelo de X?

¿Qué piensas....

¿Qué jugadores van a ser seleccionados?
¿Va a jugar X?
¿Va a estar X en forma para jugar?
¿Quién va a estar en el banquillo?
¿Quién va a ser el capitán?
¿En qué posicion va a jugar X?
¿Quién va a jugar de centrocampista?
¿Quién va a marcar un gol?
¿Quién va a ganar el partido?
¿Cuál va a ser el resultado?
¿Quién va a tener tajeta amarilla?
¿Quién va a ser el jugador más importante del partido?
¿Quién ganará la copa?
¿Qué equipo va a descender/ser relegado?
¿Qué equipo ascenderá?

31   Snakes and Ladders Games (A, B & C)

SUGGESTED LANGUAGE:

Three versions of the game are included here to practise:

A   Food, Drink, Clothes and Souvenirs
B   Weather, Injuries, and Match Events
C   Ordinal Numbers and Events

SUGGESTED ACTIVITIES:

Enlarge the boards to A3. Cut out and stick the sides of the counters together. Colour in if wished.
Play in the usual way. Roll the dice, count forward, name or respond to the item on the square. If correct, move counter.

Use the template at the back of the book to create Snakes and Ladders Games on other themes. For example:
- Dates - which country won the World Cup in which year.
- Football results.
- Items and prices.

Snakes and Ladders A

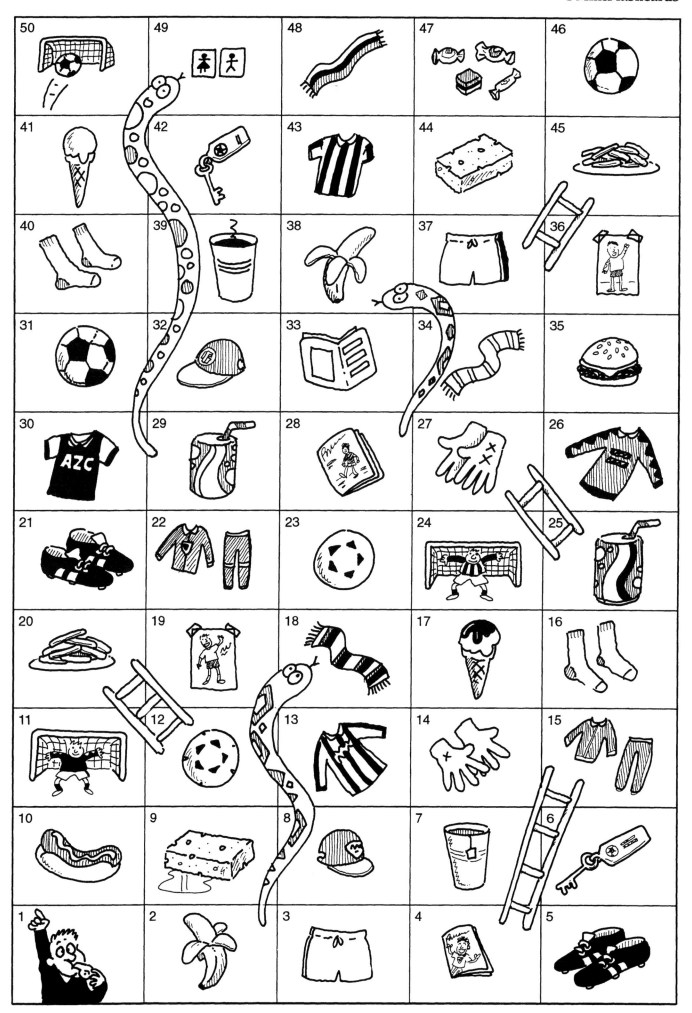

Counters:

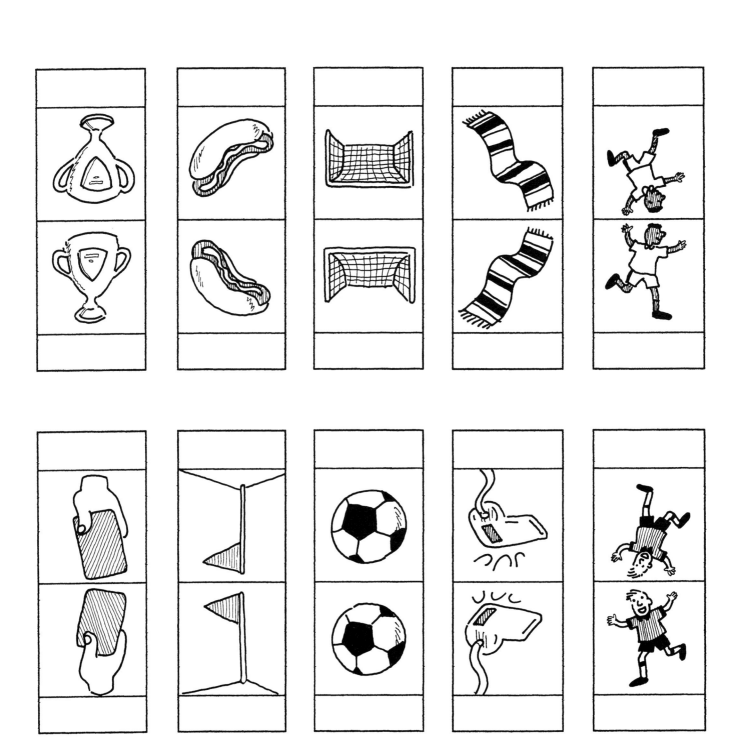

Snakes and Ladders B

50	49	48 corner! avance 2	47 expulsion! recule 4	46
41	42 carton rouge! recule 3	43	44	45
40 penalty! avance 3	39	38	37	36 coup-franc! avance 1
31	32	33 carton jaune! recule 2	34	35
30 faute! recule 1	29	28	27	26 arrêt! avance 1
21 coup-franc! avance 1	22	23	24 carton rouge! recule 3	25
20	19 but! avance 3	18 penalty! avance 3	17	16
11	12	13	14 carton jaune! recule 2	15
10 expulsion! recule 4	9	8 but! avance 3	7	6
1	2 faute! recule 1	3 corner! avance 2	4	5 arrêt! avance 1

33 Snakes and ladders (C) - Ordinal Numbers

SUGGESTED LANGUAGE:

A la septième minute (...X marque un but fabuleux, ...il y a un penalty...)
In the 7th minute (...X scores a great goal, ...there's a penalty...)

Game Variation: Each time a player lands on a square, s/he scores a goal *(A la septième minute je marque un but fabuleux.)* A record is kept of the number of goals scored. The aim is to reach top as slowly as possible and get the most goals!

premier/première	*first*
deuxième	*second*
troisième	*third*
quatrième	*fourth*
cinquième	*fifth*
sixième	*sixth*
septième	*seventh*
huitième	*eighth*
neuvième	*ninth*
dixième	*tenth*
onzième	*eleventh*
douzième	*twelfth*
treizième	*thirteenth*
quatorzième	*fourteenth*
quinzième	*fifteenth*
seizième	*sixteenth*
dix-septième	*seventeenth*
dix-huitième	*eighteenth*
dix-neuvième	*nineteenth*
vingtième	*twentieth*
vingt et unième	*twenty first*
vingt-deuxième	*twenty second*
vingt-troisième	*twenty third*
trentième	*thirtieth*
trente et unième	*thirty first*
trente-deuxième	*thirty second*
trente-troisième	*thirty third*
quarantième	*fortieth*
quarante et unième	*forty first*
quarante-deuxième	*forty second*
quarante-quatrième	*forty fourth*
cinquantième	*fiftieth*
cinquante et unième	*fifty first*
cinquante-deuxième	*fifty second*
cinquante-cinquième	*fifty fifth*
soixantième	*sixtieth*
soixante et unième	*sixty first*
soixante-deuxième	*sixty second*
soixante-sixième	*sixty sixth*
soixante-dixième	*seventieth*
soixante et onzième	*seventy first*
soixante-douzième	*seventy second*
soixante-seizième	*seventy sixth*
soixante-dix-septième	*seventy seventh*
quatre-vingtième	*eightieth*
quatre-vingt-unième	*eighty first*
quatre-vingt-deuxième	*eighty second*
quatre-vingt-huitième	*eighty eighth*
quatre-vingt-neuvième	*eighty ninth*
quatre-vingt-dixième	*ninetieth*

Snakes and Ladders C

90e	89e	88e	82e	81e
71e	72e	76e	77e	80e
70e	66e	62e	61e	60e
44e	50e	51e	52e	55e
42e	41e	40e	33e	32e
21e	22e	23e	30e	31e
20e	19e	18e	17e	16e
11e	12e	13e	14e	15e
10e	9e	8e	7e	6e
1ère	2e	3e	4e	5e

34   At the Match - Spot the Difference

Au match

Spot the Differences between the local game and the big media event!

SUGGESTED LANGUAGE:

A:

Il pleut	*It's raining*
Ça fait zéro - zéro	*The score's 0-0*
Il est quatre heures cinq	*It's five minutes past four*
Un joueur discute avec l'arbitre	*One player is arguing with the ref*
L'arbitre prend son nom	*The referee is booking him*
Deux joueurs se battent	*Two players are fighting*
Un joueur prend une boisson	*One player is having a drink*
Un joueur reçoit des soins du kinésithérapeute	*The physio is attending to one player*
On sort du terrain un joueur sur un brancard	*One player is being carried off the field*
Le gardien de but lit un journal	*The keeper is reading a newspaper*
Il y a trois spectateurs dont un chien	*There are 3 spectators including a dog*
Les spectateurs s'ennuient	*The spectators are bored*

B:

Il fait du soleil	*It's sunny*
Ça fait cinq - trois	*The score's five - three*
Il y a un grand tableau d'affichage	*There's a big scoreboard*
Il est trois heures dix	*It's ten past three*
Un joueur vient de marquer un but	*One player has just scored*
Un joueur saute de joie	*One player is jumping for joy*
Un joueur est bouleversé	*One player is in despair*
Deux joueurs s'étreignent	*Two players are hugging each other*
Il y a un juge de touche	*There's an assistant referee*
Un photographe prend une photo	*A photographer's taking a picture*
Il y a un policier	*There's a police officer*
Il y a beaucoup de spectateurs	*There's a big crowd*
Les spectateurs sont en extase	*The fans are over the moon*

Plus describe:
- What players look like, of various ages/fitness levels.
- The various styles of kit.

ADDITIONAL ACTIVITIES:

- Selected activities from Unit 2. Beat the Clock - naming items, or verbs. I Spy...
- Imagine what people are saying or thinking.
- Cut out pictures from football magazines to make your own Spot the Difference.

At the Match - Spot the Difference

Le Football (A)

Look at the pictures below. Find and mark the matching French words hidden in the grid, then label the pictures correctly.

_____ _____ _____

 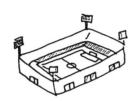  

_____ _____ _____

Y	À	H	H	U	F	A	I	F	Ï	I	Ç
À	Û	H	T	Ê	D	S	Ç	J	Ô	Î	U
S	S	N	Z	W	M	T	O	W	L	X	R
Î	T	Z	T	Ê	Q	U	L	M	À	Y	Ç
X	A	R	N	A	E	B	V	A	I	S	N
H	D	È	G	U	V	B	É	I	O	O	D
R	E	P	R	A	H	C	É	L	L	B	O
B	P	Y	B	Ê	R	C	H	L	È	B	O
È	I	E	A	O	D	D	A	O	Ç	P	T
Î	U	Ç	Û	A	R	B	I	T	R	E	Q
À	Q	V	S	I	F	F	L	E	T	Q	C
Q	É	G	X	Ô	P	H	D	I	N	N	X

_____

_____

Le Football (B)

Twenty-four French words associated with football are hidden in the grid.
Find them, mark them, and write them down in the list

le _____ football

le _____ stadium

le _____ football shirt

l' _____ team

le _____ goal

la _____ stand

le _____ spectator

la _____ cup

la _____ mascot

l' _____ referee

l' _____ trainer

le _____ player

le _____ substitute

le _____ captain

le _____ shorts

le _____ ball

le _____ fan

le _____ ground

le _____ net

la _____ crossbar

l' _____ wing

le _____ bench

le _____ whistle

le _____ championship

O	W	H	L	S	T	R	O	H	S	M	É	Ï	E
L	V	Ê	Î	C	H	E	K	U	A	L	Ô	G	N
V	Ç	E	C	H	A	M	P	I	O	N	N	A	T
M	A	Û	Q	R	C	P	L	I	U	B	B	L	R
B	X	C	U	O	O	L	I	T	U	A	O	N	A
Ê	I	H	U	R	O	A	S	T	L	Q	E	I	Î
Î	K	P	T	T	Û	Ç	Î	L	A	T	É	A	N
E	E	E	T	C	K	A	O	U	T	I	F	R	E
É	R	N	R	Ï	N	N	Ô	O	Ô	R	N	R	U
Û	R	U	E	T	A	T	C	E	P	S	T	E	R
A	A	B	E	D	I	S	I	F	F	L	E	T	Ê
A	B	I	Û	U	A	B	A	N	C	F	L	O	D
È	L	R	L	M	O	T	R	H	L	Z	I	O	E
Q	D	T	Î	E	Û	J	S	A	E	I	F	F	B

For solutions see Unit 60

37   Quiz Questions

There is much scope in football for quiz questions of different grades of difficulty. Various formats can be used including Multiple Choice, True or False, Odd One Out or Open Ended. If any of the first three, they can become self access reading and listening activities.

NB **Topical Questions** - Some kinds of questions will date - learners can very easily devise their own topical questions, based on model formats.
Quel est le nom du gardien blessé actuellement?
Quelle sorte de blessure?

Some examples are given on the themes of Number, Colour and Players. The Players' questions are examples only, without answers, as these questions will date.
Examples of the very many other types of questions are:

Simple Vocabulary Games

Dates (Past/Future Tenses)
Quelle équipe a gagné la Coupe du Monde en 1994?
OR En quelle année l'équipe d'Angleterre a gagné la Coupe du Monde?
En quelle année se passera la prochaine Coupe du Monde?

Past Tense
Qui a joué contre MU samedi dernier?
Qui a gagné?
Quel était le score?
Qui a marqué les buts?
Qui a été expulsé?
Qui était le gardien de but de MU?
Quel temps faisait-il?

Future Tense
MU va jouer contre quelle équipe ce week-end?
Qui va être le gardien de but de MU?
Où vont-ils jouer?
Le coup d'envoi sera à quelle heure?

Comparisons
Quel est le plus grand stade - Old Trafford ou Wembley?

Geography
Zagreb est la capitale de quel pays qui participe à la Coupe du Monde?

Miscellaneous
Quel est le surnom (nickname) de Manchester United?
A quelle heure est...(Match of the Day/Le Match du Jour)?
Sur quelle chaîne?

Statistics
Quel joueur a marqué le plus grand nombre de buts au Championnat?

Nationalité
Quelle est la nationalité de...?

Picture Questions
Cut out some magazine photos - block out the faces - *Qui est-ce?*

Who am I?
Give a few details, one at a time, about eg age, team, hair colour, engaged to, husband of...

Odd One Out
Qui ne joue pas pour L'Equipe de X.., pour l'Angleterre..?

Les Nombres

Il y a combien de joueurs dans une équipe?

Huit

Onze

Treize

Les Nombres

Il y a combien de gardiens de but dans une équipe?

Un

Deux

Quatre

Les Nombres

Il y a combien de minutes dans un match?

Soixante

Quatre-vingt-dix

Cent

Les Nombres

Il y a combien d'arbitres dans un match?

Un

Trois

Cinq

Les Nombres

Il y a combien de juges de touche dans un match?

Un

Deux

Six

Les Nombres

Il y a combien de joueurs dans une équipe?

Huit

Onze

Treize

Les Nombres

Il y a combien de joueurs dans un match?

Onze

Quinze

Vingt-deux

Les Nombres

Il y a combien d'équipes dans La Coupe du Monde?

Vingt-huit

Trente-deux

Trente-six

Les Nombres

L'arbitre a combien de cartons dans sa poche?

Un

Deux

Trois

Les Couleurs

De quelle couleur est la pelouse?

Noire

Rouge

Verte

Les Couleurs

De quelle couleur est la ligne?

Noire

Verte

Blanche

Les Couleurs

De quelle couleur est la boue?

Brune

Rouge

Jaune

Les Couleurs

De quelle couleur est la neige?

Rouge

Blanche

Noire

Les Couleurs

De quelle couleur est le ciel?

Rouge/Blanc

Bleu/Vert

Bleu/Gris

Les Couleurs

De quelles couleurs sont les cartons de l'arbitre?

Jaunes/Noirs

Rouges/Jaunes

Rouges/Noirs

Les Couleurs

En quelle couleur est habillé l'arbitre?

Noir

Bleu

Rouge

Les Couleurs

De quelle couleur est la tenue d'Espagne?

Bleue/Blanche

Rouge/Jaune

Rouge/Bleue

Les Couleurs

De quelle couleur est la tenue d'Italie?

Rouge/Blanche

Verte/Rouge

Blanche/Bleue

Les Joueurs

Quel est le nom du gardien de but de Manchester?

Les Joueurs

Quel est le club actuel de Bergkamp?

Les Joueurs

Quel est le club actuel de Gascoigne?

Les Joueurs

Quel est le club actuel de Ginola?

Les Joueurs

Quel est le nom de l'attaquant français qui joue pour Tottenham?

Les Joueurs

Quel est le nom de l'attaquant de Manchester commençant par la lettre G?

Les Joueurs

Quel est le nom du milieu de terrain de Manchester commençant par la lettre B?

Les Joueurs

Qui est le joueur le plus jeune de l'équipe d'Angleterre?

Les Joueurs

Quel est le nom du français qui était le capitaine de Manchester ?

38   Tactics! - Framework Game

La tactique!

To add to the fun of a quiz game, framework visuals or games can be used to indicate progress through the quiz. Some examples appropriate to football are offered.

TACTICS!

Photocopy the board. Enlarge to A3 if preferred. (Or play on the blackboard or OHP as a team game)
The board represents two possible team formations on a pitch: 4 - 4 - 2 and 5 - 3 - 2.

Each Team has 1 or 2 players.
Each team has 3 balls (counters).

Les capitaines tirent à pile ou face.
Le gagnant donne le coup d'envoi.
L'autre choisit un côté ou une formation.

The captains toss a coin.
The winner kicks off.
The loser chooses an end/formation

L'équipe A répond à une question. S'ils ont raison, ils avancent le ballon d'un pas vers le but de l'autre côté.
Puis c'est le tour de l'équipe B.
Le but du jeu, c'est d'être le premier à marquer trois buts.
Il n'est pas permis de se placer sur une position déjà occupée.

Team A answers a quiz question. If they get it right, they move one place forward towards the goal at the other end.
Then it is the turn of Team B.
The aim is to be the first to score all three goals at the other end (ie get their counters into the goal)
A ball may not move to an occupied position.

Longer Game - each team has 4 or 5 balls (counters) to score goals with depending on time available.
Or remove some of the positions.

Other simple visual devices:

- Draw a number of balls on the board as in a penalty shoot-out.
- Use the illustration of the pitch in Unit 40 and section off segments to indicate progression towards a goal.
- Use a knock out system - last eight players up to the final.

Tactics!

© MiniFlashcards

39 Features of the Pitch

Le Terrain de jeu

On the pitch. Key features.

SUGGESTED LANGUAGE:

1. the pitch	1. le terrain de jeu	1. das Spielfeld	1. el campo
2. the ground/ the grass	2. le sol/la pelouse	2. der Boden/Rasen	2. el terreno/el césped
3. the (touch) line	3. la ligne (de touche)	3. die Linie	3. la linea de fondo
4. the corner/the corner flag	4. le coin/le drapeau de coin/le corner	4. die Ecke/ dieEckfahne	4. el saque de esquina/banderín de esquina
5. the goal	5. les buts m / les cages f	5. das Tor	5. el gol
6. the net	6. le filet	6. das Netz	6. la red
7. the goal post	7. le poteau/ le montant	7. der Torpfosten	7. el poste de la portería
8. the crossbar	8. la barre/la (barre) transversale	8. die Querlatte	8. el largero
9. goal line	9. la ligne de but	9. die Torlinie	9. la línea de gol
10. central circle	10. le rond central	10. der Mittelkreis	10. el círculo central
11. penalty area	11. la surface de réparation	11. der Strafraum	11. el área pequeña
12. penalty spot	12. le point de réparation/de penalty	12. der Elfmeterpunkt	12. el punto de penalty

ADDITIONAL LANGUAGE:

1. la surface de but	1. goal area/box
2. l'aile f	2. wing
3. le milieu de terrain	3. halfway line
4. avant	4. downfield
5. arrière	5. upfield
6. le banc	6. the bench

SUGGESTED ACTIVITIES:

- Selected games from Unit 2.
- Discussion - *Doit-on agrandir les buts ?*

Features of the Pitch

40   The Pitch

SUGGESTED LANGUAGE:

See previous Unit 39.

SUGGESTED ACTIVITIES:

- Enlarge to A3 if wished.
- Photocopy and label the pitch. Research and include dimensions. Or draw your own version.
- Draw and label your Dream Team in their positions. Include also the referee, assistants, photographers etc, either drawn or pasted up from illustrations in other Units.
- Then selected activities from Unit 2 eg True or False. I Went to Market, Beat the Clock.

The Pitch - Plan

© MiniFlashcards

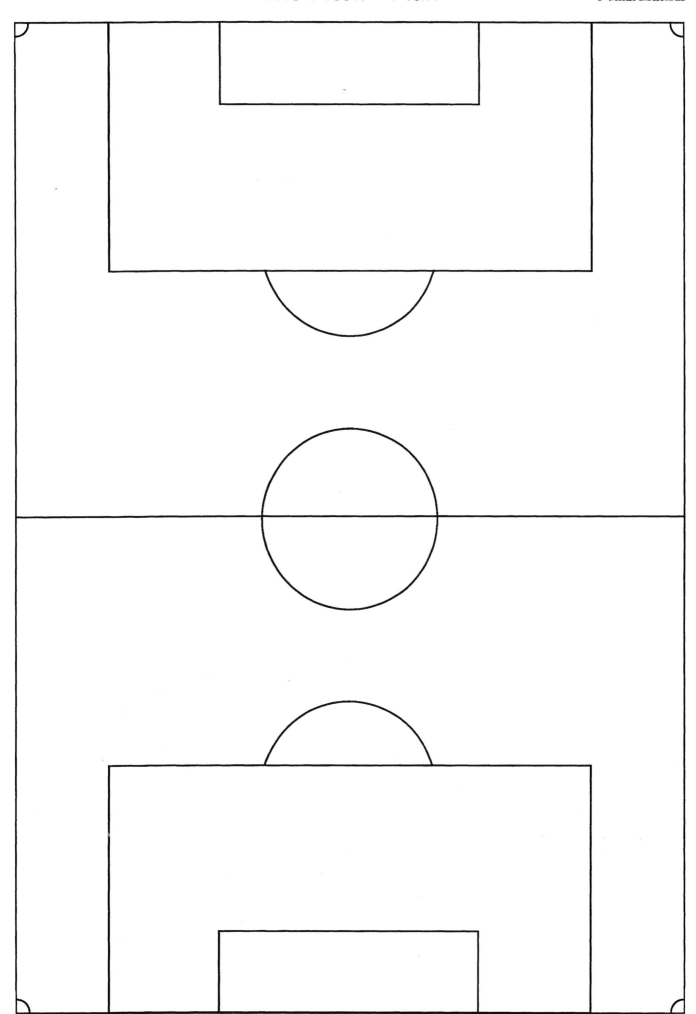

41   Things on the Pitch

Sur le terrain

SUGGESTED LANGUAGE:

1. band	1. l'orchestre m	1. die Band/ (Musik)Kapelle	1. la orquesta
2. mascot	2. la mascotte	2. das Maskottchen	2. la mascota
3. coin	3. la pièce (de monnaie)	3. die Münze	3. la moneda
4. whistle	4. le sifflet	4. die Pfeife	4. el silbato
5. ball	5. le ballon	5. der Ball	5. el bálon
6. assistant referee's flag	6. le drapeau du juge de touche	6. die Fahne des Linienrichters	6. la bandera del juez de línea
7. red/yellow card	7. le carton rouge/jaune	7. die rote/gelbe Karte	7. la tarjeta roja/amarilla
8. referee's book	8. le carnet de l'arbitre	8. das Buch des Schiedsrichters	8. la libreta del árbitro
9. pencil	9. le crayon	9. der Bleistift	9. el lápiz
10. drink	10. la boisson	10. das Getränk	10. la bebida
11. watch	11. la montre	11. die Armbanduhr	11. el reloj
12. trophy	12. le trophée	12. der Pokal	12. el trofeo

ADDITIONAL LANGUAGE:

1. l'orchestre quitte le terrain	1. the band's going off the pitch
2. le supporteur agite/brandit la mascotte	2. the fan's waving the mascot
3. l'arbitre tire à pile ou face	3. the referee's tossing the coin
4. l'arbitre donne un coup de sifflet	4. the referee blows his whistle
5. le joueur tire le ballon	5. the player kicks the ball
6. l'arbitre regarde sa montre	6. the referee looks at his watch
7. l'arbitre sort son carnet et son crayon	7. the referee's getting out his book/pencil
8. l'arbitre élève un carton rouge/jaune	8. the referee's holding up a red/yellow card
9. le juge de touche agite son drapeau	9. the assistant referee's waving his flag
10. le joueur prend une boisson	10. the player's having a drink
11. l'arbitre siffle la mi-temps	11. the referee blows his whistle for half-time
12. l'arbitre siffle une faute	12. the referee whistles for a foul
13. le capitaine brandit le trophée	13. the captain's holds up the trophy

SUGGESTED ACTIVITIES:

- Selected activities from Unit 2, eg I Went to Market, Sequencing, Kim's Game, Beat the Clock.
- Make up a commentary in the past tense, with timings.

Things on the Pitch

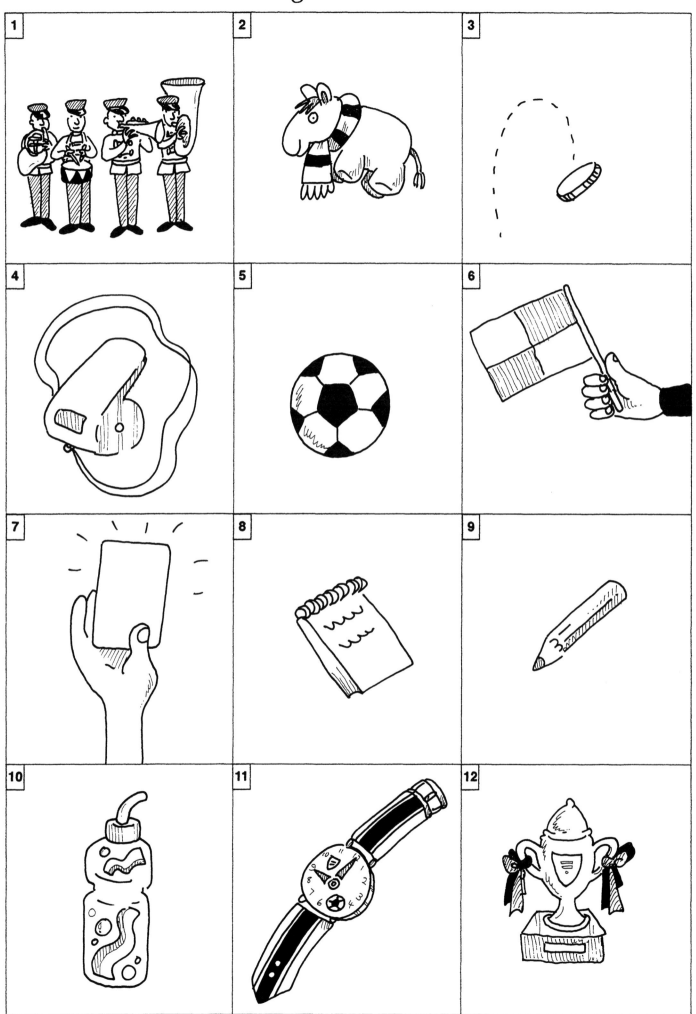

42 The Game - Organisation

L'organisation du jeu

SUGGESTED LANGUAGE:

1. the kick-off	1. le coup d'envoi	1. der Anstoß/Anpfiff	1. el saque inicial
2. half-time	2. la mi-temps	2. die Halbzeit	2. el descanso de
3. full-time	3. la fin de/du match	3. das Spielende	medio tiempo
4. a goal	4. un but marqué/	4. das Tor	3. el fin del partido
5. a penalty	un but	5. der Elfmeter	4. un gol
6. an own goal	5. un coup de pied de	6. ein Eigentor	5. un penalty
7. the score	réparation (un	7. der Punktestand/	6. un autogol
8. a win	penalty)	das Ergebnis	7. el marcador
9. a defeat	6. un but contre son	8. ein Sieg	8. una victoria
10. a draw	camp	9. ein verlorenes	9. una derrota
11. extra time/injury	7. le score	Spiel	10. un empate
time/stoppage	8. une victoire	10. ein	11 la prórroga/ el
12. penalty shoot out	9. une défaite	unentschiedenes	tiempo añadido/
/sudden death	10. un match nul	Spiel	descuento
	11. les prolongations	11. Verlängerung f	12. una tanda de
	fpl	12. Elfmeterschießen	penaltis / la muerte
	12. une série de tirs au		súbita
	but /la mort subite		

ADDITIONAL LANGUAGE:

1. le coup d'envoi est à 15h	1. the kick-off's at 3pm
2. à quelle heure ça démarre?	2. when's the kick-off?
3. où en est le match?/quel est le score?	3. what's the score?
4. ça fait (trois-un à...)	4. it's (three-one to....)
5. le but égalisateur	5. equaliser
6. un match à domicile	6. home match
7. un match à l'extérieur	7. away match
8. la finale	8. final
9. la demi-finale	9. semi final
10. le quart de finale	10. quarter final
11. la ligue	11. league
12. la division	12. division
13. le match rejoué	13. replay
14. le championnat	14. championship
15. suspendu	15. suspended
16. faire un changement	16. make a substitution

Approximate tournament equivalents:

1. la Coupe de la Ligue	1. the League Cup
2. la Coupe de France	2. the FA Cup
3. la Ligue des Champions	3. the Champions League
4. la Coupe des Coupes	4. the Cup Winners' Cup
5. la Coupe de L'UEFA	5. the UEFA Cup
6. la Coupe du Monde/Le Mondial	6. the World Cup

SUGGESTED ACTIVITIES:

- Selected activities from Unit 2.
- Combine with other Units eg 41-44 to make up Match Reports.

The Game - Organisation

43 The Game - Technical

La technique du jeu

1. (to make) a short pass	1. (faire) une passe courte	1. einen kurzen Paß spielen	1. (hacer) un pase corto
2. (to make) a long pass	2. (faire) une passe longue	2. einen langen Paß spielen	2. (hacer) un pase largo
3. (to) (a) dribble	3. le dribble/dribbler	3. dribbeln	3. regatear
4. (to take) a shot at goal/shoot (to score) a goal	4. tirer au but (marquer) un but	4. auf das Tor schießen	4. marcar un gol
5. (to head the ball) a header	5. (faire/donner) une tête	5. ein Kopfball	5. cebecear
6. (to take) a free kick	6. (tirer) un coup franc	6. einen Freistoß spielen	6. (hacer) un libre directo
7. (to take) a throw-in	7. (faire) une touche/jouer la touche	7. einen Einwurf machen	7. (hacer) un saque de banda
8. (to take) a goal kick	8. (faire) un coup de pied de but/un dégagement	8. einen Schuß auf's Tor machen	8. (hacer) un saque de portería
9. (to take) a corner	9. (tirer) un corner	9. einen Eckstoß machen	9. (tirar) un saque de esquina

ADDITIONAL LANGUAGE:

1. marquer (ton/son adversaire)	1. to mark (your opponent)
2. marquer X de très près	2. to mark X very closely
3. la défense individuelle	3. man-to-man marking
4. la défense de zone	4. zonal marking
5. tacler	5. to tackle
6. défendre le but	6. to defend the goal
7. sauver un but	7. to make a save
8. faire un plongeon	8. to dive
9. faire une (reprise de) volée	9. to volley (the ball)
10. rechercher (de) l'espace	10. to look for a space
11. appeler le ballon	11. to call for the ball
12. chercher	12. to look for
13. trouver	13. to find
14. entrer en collision avec	14. to collide with
15. dégager le ballon	15. to clear the ball
16. intercepter une passe	16. to intercept a pass
17. repousser/détourner le ballon	17. to knock away the ball
18. être hors-jeu	18. to be off-side
19. dans le football, ce qui compte c'est de marquer des buts, rien d'autre!	19. soccer is all about scoring goals, nothing else!
20. des buts font des victoires!	20. goals win games!

SUGGESTED ACTIVITIES:

- Selected games from Unit 2.
- Make up short phrases for a commentary. Link the events. Combine with items from other units.
- Watch a video, pause it, make a comment.
- Video a school match and make up a commentary.

The Game - Technical

44   Foul !

Fautes!

SUGGESTED LANGUAGE:

Il ne faut pas...

1. *donner un coup de pied à un adversaire*
2. *faire un croche-pied à un adversaire*
3. *sauter sur ou par-dessus un adversaire*
4. *bousculer/charger violemment ou dangereusement un adversaire*
5. *charger un adversaire par derrière/pousser dans le dos*
6. *frapper un adversaire/donner une gifle à...*
7. *(re)tenir un adversaire/tirer le maillot*
8. *pousser un adversaire*
9. *toucher le ballon avec les mains/faire une main (sauf pour le gardien de but dans la surface de réparation)*

Man darf nicht ...

1. *seinen Gegner treten*
2. *seinem Gegner ein Bein stellen*
3. *über seinen Gegner springen*
4. *seinen Gegner angehen*
5. *einen Gegner von hinten schubsen*
6. *einen Gegner schlagen*
7. *einen Gegner zurückhalten*
8. *einen Gegner schubsen*
9. *den Ball mit der Hand berühren (abgesehen vom Torwart im Strafraum)*

You can't...

1. *kick an opponent*
2. *trip up ....*
3. *jump over...*
4. *charge into...*
5. *shove... from behind*
6. *hit...*
7. *hold back...*
8. *push...*
9. *touch the ball with your hand/do a hand ball (except for the goalkeeper in the penalty area)*

No puedes...

1. *dar una patada a un oponente*
2. *poner la zancadilla...*
3. *saltar sobre el adversario*
4. *cargar contra...*
5. *empujar... por detrás*
6. *golpear...*
7. *retener... al adversario*
8. *empujar a...*
   tocar la pelota con las manos (excepto el portero en el área)

ADDITIONAL LANGUAGE:

1. *X a donné un coup de pied à Y*
2. *X a fait un croche-pied à Y*
3. *X a chargé Y par derrière*
4. *X a frappé Y*
5. *X a touché la balle avec les mains/a fait une main*
6. *(c'est) main!*
7. *il a commis/fait une faute*
8. *l'arbitre a pris son nom*
9. *le joueur a discuté avec l'arbitre*
10. *il lui a montré un carton jaune/rouge*
11. *il l'a expulsé*

1. *X kicked Y*
2. *X tripped Y up*
3. *X shoved Y from behind*
4. *X hit Y*
5. *X did a hand ball*
6. *hand ball!*
7. *he committed a foul/he fouled*
8. *the referee booked him*
9. *the player argued with the ref*
10. *he showed him a yellow/red card*
11. *he sent him off*

SUGGESTED ACTIVITIES:

- Selected games from Unit 2.
- Watch a football video. Count the number of fouls in a 10 minute period of a game, or complete match, and list them in a chart.

Foul!

45 Some of the Rules - True/False

Quelques règles

A few of the rules of the game, simplified: (refer to a rule book for the full rules).

SUGGESTED LANGUAGE:

1. *Il y a onze joueurs.*
   N'importe quel joueur peut remplacer le gardien de but.
   Un joueur expulsé par l'arbitre ne peut être remplacé.

2. *Le gardien de but doit avoir une tenue d'une couleur différente de celle des autres joueurs.*
   La couleur noire est réservée à l'arbitre.
   Le cuissard doit être de la même couleur que le short.

3. *Les décisions de l'arbitre sont sans appel.*
   Les juges de touche agitent des drapeaux pour signaler un hors-jeu ou une faute.

4. *Il y a 2 périodes de 45 minutes, avec une pause entre les 2 mi-temps.*
   Plus des prolongations pour des arrêts de jeu.
   Quelquefois - des prolongations après un match nul - 2 fois 15 minutes.
   Puis une série de tirs au but - la mort subite.

5. *Le carton jaune signifie un avertissement.*
   Le carton rouge signifie une exclusion.
   L'arbitre siffle un penalty lorsqu'une faute est commise dans la surface de réparation.

6. *Il y a un coup de pied de but lorsque le ballon est touché par un attaquant avant de franchir la ligne de but.*
   Il y a un corner lorsque le ballon est touché par un défenseur avant de franchir la ligne de but.

---

1. *There are eleven players.*
   Any player can replace the goalkeeper.
   A player who has been sent off cannot be replaced.

2. *The goalkeeper has to wear kit of a different colour to that of the other players.*
   The colour black is reserved for the referee.
   Cycle shorts have to be the same colour as the shorts.

3. *The decision of the referee is final.*
   The assistant referees wave their flag to indicate an off-side or foul.

4. *There are 2 periods of 45 minutes, with a break between the 2 halves.*
   Plus extra time for stoppages.
   Sometimes extra time for a draw - 15 minutes each way.
   Then a penalty shoot-out - sudden death.

5. *The yellow card means a warning.*
   The red card means a sending-off.
   The referee awards a penalty when there is a foul in the penalty area.

6. *There is a goal kick when the ball is touched by an attacker before crossing the goal line.*
   There is a corner when the ball is touched by a defender before crossing the goal line.

SUGGESTED ACTIVITIES:

- Choose some statements and amend certain of them. Create a True or False Quiz.

46 Vital Statistics!

Quelques chiffres For those keen on football stats!

SUGGESTED LANGUAGE:

nombre de buts inscrits	*number of goals scored*
nombre de buts encaissés	*number of goals conceded*
nombre de buts contre son camp	*number of own goals*
nombre de corners	*number of corners*
nombre de fautes	*number of fouls*
nombre de penalties	*number of penalties*
nombre d'avertissements	*number of warnings*
nombre de cartons jaunes	*number of yellow cards*
nombre de cartons rouges/d'expulsions (avec noms)	*number of red cards/expulsions (with names)*
nombre de buts de la tête	*number of goals scored with a header*
nombre de buts du pied droit	*number of goals scored with the right foot*
nombre de buts du pied gauche	*number of goals scored with the left foot*
nombre de buts marqués sur coups francs	*number of goals scored from a free kick*
nombre de buts marqués sur corner	*number of goals scored from a corner*
nombre de points	*number of points*
nombre de journées en dernière position	*number of days at the bottom of the division*
nombre de journées passées en tête	*number of days at the top of the division*
moyenne de buts par match	*average number of goals scored per match*
le meilleur buteur de tous les temps	*the top goal scorer of all time*
le meilleur buteur sur une saison	*the top goal scorer in a season*
le meilleur buteur sur un match	*the top goal scorer in a match*

Anzahl der geschossenen Tore	*número de goles marcados*
Anzahl der Gegentore	*número de goles concedidos*
Anzahl der Eigentore	*número de autogoles*
Anzahl der Ecken	*número de saques de esquina*
Anzahl der Fouls	*número de faltas*
Anzahl der Elfmeter	*número de penaltis*
Anzahl der Verwarnungen	*número de advertencias*
Anzahl der gelben Karten	*número de tarjetas amarillas*
Anzahl der roten Karten/Platzverweise (mit Namen)	*número de tarjetas rojas expulsiones (con nombre)*
Anzahl der durch Kopfschuß erzielten Tore	*número de goles marcados con la cabeza*
Anzahl der mit dem rechten Fuß geschossenen Tore	*número de goles marcados con el pie derecho*
Anzahl der mit dem linken Fuß geschossenen Tore	*número de goles marcados con el pie izquierdo*
Anzahl der durch einen Freistoß erzielten Tore	*número de goles marcados de libre directo*
Anzahl der durch einen Eckstoß erzielten Tore	*número de goles marcados desde un saque de esquina*
Punktestand	*número de puntos*
Anzahl der Tage ganz unten in der Liga	*número de días en la posición más baja de la división?*
Anzahl der Tage ganz oben in der Liga	*número de días a la cabeza de la división?*
Durchschnittszahl der pro Spiel geschossenen Tore	*media del número de goles marcados por partido*
der Torschützenkönig aller Zeiten	*el mejor goleador de todos los tiempos*
der Torschützenkönig der Saison	*el mejor goleador de la temporada*
der Torschützenkönig des Spiels	*el mejor goleador en un partido*

SUGGESTED ACTIVITIES:

- From a selection of football results over a period of time, draw up charts for the above.

47 My Afternoon at the Match - Story

Mon après-midi au match

1. J'ai quitté la maison à 2h
2. J'ai pris le bus
3. Je suis arrivé(e) au stade à 2h 20
4. J'ai acheté un billet
5. J'ai acheté un programme
6. J'ai bu un coca
7. J'ai trouvé ma place
8. Ipswich a marqué un but
9. A la mi-temps, j'ai mangé un hamburger
10. J'ai repris ma place
11. Manchester a commis une faute dans la surface de réparation
12. Ipswich a transformé le penalty
13. L'arbitre a expulsé un joueur de Manchester
14. Ipswich a marqué un troisième but
15. Ipswich a gagné 3-0
16. Les supporters étaient ravis!

1. I left home at 2pm
2. I caught the bus
3. I arrived at the stadium at 2.20pm
4. I bought a ticket
5. I bought a programme
6. I drank a coke
7. I found my seat
8. Ipswich got a goal
9. At half-time I had a burger
10. I took my seat again
11. Manchester committed a foul in the penalty area
12. Ipswich got the penalty
13. The referee sent off a player from Manchester
14. Ipswich got a third goal
15. Ipswich won 3-0
16. The fans were over the moon!

1. Ich bin um 14 Uhr aus dem Haus gegangen.
2. Ich bin mit dem Bus gefahren.
3. Ich bin um 14.20 Uhr am Stadion angekommen.
4. Ich habe eine Eintrittskarte gekauft.
5. Ich habe ein Programm gekauft.
6. Ich habe eine Cola getrunken.
7. Ich habe meinen Platz gefunden/Ich bin auf meinen Platz gegangen.
8. Ipswich hat ein Tor geschossen.
9. Zur Halbzeit habe ich einen Hamburger gegessen.
10. Ich bin wieder auf meinen Platz gegangen.
11. Manchester hat ein Foul in der Elfmeterzone begangen.
12. Ipswich hat den Elfmeter verwandelt.
13. Der Schiedsrichter hat einen Manchesterspieler des Platzes verwiesen.
14. Ipswich hat noch ein Tor geschossen.
15. Ipswich hat 3-0 gewonnen.
16. Die Fans waren vor Freude außer sich.

1. Salí de casa a las 2 pm
2. Cogí el autobús
3. Llegué al estadio a las 2.20 pm
4. Compré una entrada
5. Compré un programa
6. Bebí una coca cola
7. Encontré mi sitio
8. Ipswich marcó un gol
9. En el descanso comí una hamburguesa
10. Fui a mi sitio otra vez
11. El Manchester cometió una falta en el área pequeña
14. Ipswich marcó un tercer gol
15 Ipswich ganó 3-0
16 Los aficionados estaban locos de alegría.

La Olla des spectateurs! - Mexican Wave

- Selected activities from Unit 2.
- Write a story of a bad day at the match:
  Problems with weather, transport, tickets, programmes, seat, dreadful match, dreadful food..., the captain argued with the referee and got sent off, the team lost, the fans were fed up!

My Afternoon at the Match

48　Our Saturday Game - Story

Notre match du samedi

SUGGESTED LANGUAGE:

1. *Quelquefois on a de la chance et il y a du soleil!*
2. *Les adultes doivent être défenseurs, parce que nous, les enfants, préférons être attaquants - nous adorons tirer au but!*
3. *Les adultes sont aussi les arbitres - et ils se disputent toujours!*
4. *Nous les enfants aimons courir avec le ballon sous les arbres - les adultes ne peuvent pas nous suivre!*
5. *Il y a toujours beaucoup de collisions!*
6. *On tombe souvent dans la boue!*
7. *Il y a toujours un joueur très doué! Personne ne peut l'attraper/l'arrêter!*
8. *D'habitude quelqu'un envoie le ballon dans la rivière!*
9. *Aïe! Les adultes essaient de le rattraper à l'aide de branches.*
10. *Quelquefois il faut courir jusqu'au pont pour le rattraper.*
11. *Quelquefois il y a beaucoup de vent et des nuages.*
12. *Des fois, il pleut - les adultes veulent s'arrêter - mais nous les enfants voulons continuer!*
13. *A la fin, nous sommes tous couverts de boue!*
14. *Une des mamans vient chercher son fils - elle a deux chiens mignons.*
15. *Mais un des chiens fait toujours pipi sur les sacs et il faut le chasser!*
16. *On s'amuse toujours bien le samedi matin au match!*

1. *Sometimes we're lucky and the sun shines!*
2. *The adults have to be defenders, because we kids prefer to be attackers - we love shooting at goal!*
3. *The adults are also the referees - and they always argue!*
4. *We kids like to run under the trees with the ball, so the adults can't follow!*
5. *There are always lots of pile-ups!*
6. *We fall in the mud a lot!*
7. *There's always one very good player - no-one can catch him!*
8. *Usually someone kicks the ball in the river.*
9. *Then the adults try to catch the ball with sticks.*
10. *Sometimes you have to run down to the bridge to stop it.*
11. *Sometimes it's quite windy with lots of clouds*
12. *Sometimes it rains - the adults want to stop - we kids want to go on!*
13. *By the end we're all covered in mud!*
14. *One mother comes to collect her son - she has two cute dogs.*
15. *But one of the dogs always cocks its leg over the bags and you have to shoo it away!*
16. *We always have a great time on Saturday mornings at the game!*

SUGGESTED ACTIVITIES:

- Selected activities from Unit 2.
- Convert the story into the past tense.
- Describe the scene - weather, park, people, clothes, drinks, goalposts etc.
- Describe a casual game you have played or watched near where you live.

Our Saturday Game

© MiniFlashcards

49 Mood of the Match!

L'humeur du match

Football fever grips you! - mood swings from one moment to another as fortunes change!

SUGGESTED LANGUAGE:

1. confident
2. anxious, worried, tense
3. furious
4. delighted
5. shocked
6. disgusted, fed up
7. elated
8. (they're) bored
9. despairing, disappointed, frustrated

1. confiant
2. inquiet/inquiète, tendu, anxieux/euse
3. furieux/euse
4. ravi
5. secoué
6. abattu, déprimé
7. en extase
8. ils s'ennuient
9. bouleversé, désespéré, frustré, déçû

1. selbstsicher
2. ängstlich, besorgt, angespannt
3. wütend
4. glücklich
5. schockiert
6. entsetzt, die Nase voll haben
7. begeistert
8. gelangweilt
9. verzweifelt, enttäuscht, frustriert

1. seguro
2. agobiado, preocupado, tenso
3. furioso
4. encantado
5. recibió un choque
6. disgustado, harto
7. eufórico
8. (están) aburrido(s)
9. desesperado, decepcionado, frustrado

ADDITIONAL LANGUAGE:

1. content
2. calme
3. triomphant
4. agacé
5. fier/fière
6. bruyant
7. calme
8. sombre/morne
9. les supporters ont eu un coup terrible

1. pleased
2. calm
3. triumphant
4. annoyed
5. proud
6. noisy
7. quiet
8. gloomy
9. the fans were devastated

General Exclamations:

Aïe, oh là, oh là là

Approval/Encouragement::

Sensass! Bravo! Magnifique! Extra! Super! Formidable! Splendide! Bien fait! But! Bien défendu! Quel match! Quel arrêt! Allez! Allez les bleus! Allez la France! Allez les gars!

Disapproval:

T'es fou ou quoi? Ne fais pas ça! Tu es idiot! Impossible! Quel dommage! Mince! Mer...credi! Quelle horreur! Il faut frapper! Hélas! Attention! C'est bête! Bon à rien! Ça ne sert à rien! Oh la vache! Il n'y a personne! Pas possible! Mais qu'est-ce qu'ils font! Allez..ils s'endorment ou quoi? Et voilà! Mais non! Les joueurs ont les pieds carrés! Qu'est-ce que vous attendez? Chut! Mal joué! Dommage! Quelle patate! Et la défense, là!

SUGGESTED ACTIVITIES:

- Selected activities from Unit 2, eg Charades.
- Match the pictures to positive/negative pictures from other sections eg Foul!, Game Technique.
- Play a football video - suggest suitable expressions to match the action.
- Explain what happened to make them happy, frustrated etc.
- Complain! The captain, manager, referee should have....

Mood of the Match

50   Souvenir Order Form

Bon de commande

SUGGESTED LANGUAGE:

As on order form. Refer to Units 12, 13, 15 and 17 for items to order.

SUGGESTED ACTIVITIES:

- Complete a sample form.
- Then selected activities from Unit 2, eg Guessing Game, True or False.
- Produce a True/False Quiz based on the information on the form.
- Use as a reading exercise.
- Use as a dictionary exercise.
- Find the French for...
- Ask each other questions: *Quelle est l'adresse de...?*
- Fill out your order form. Ring the Souvenir shop and record your order on the answerphone. The shop assistant listens to the message and write it down.
- Complete one form, then copy selected items onto two others to create an information-gap exercise.

PARIS FOOT

BON DE COMMANDE

à adresser avec votre chèque bancaire ou postal libellé à l'ordre du Paris Foot, majoré de 30 F pour frais d'envoi à l'adresse ci-dessous:

BOUTIQUE PARIS FOOT
BP 236
75529 Paris
Tél: 01.23.45.67.89

Vos coordonnées

M ☐   Mme ☐   Melle ☐

Nom:_____

Prénom:_____

Adresse:_____

_____

Code postal:_____ Ville:_____

Tél: (facultatif)_____

POUR COMMANDER LA BONNE TAILLE

Age moyen	Tour de poitrine (cm)	Taille (cm)
6 ans	60	111/116
8 ans	64	117/130
10 ans	68	130/140
12 ans	75	141/152
14 ans	82	153/158
S	89	159/164
M	94	165/175
L	101	176/180
XL	106	180/185
XXL	112	+185

Example: Sweat	12/14	Bleu	0 | 0 | 2	199F 00	398F 00
Désignation des articles	**Taille**	**Couleur**	**Quantité**	**Prix unitaire**	**Prix total**
			| |		
			| |		
			| |		
			| |		
			| |		
			| |		
			| |		
			| |		
			| |		

Votre règlement:
☐ **Chèque bancaire à l'ordre du PF**
☐ **Chèque postal à l'ordre du PF**
Date et signature

Montant total	
Frais de port	**+30F**
Total à payer	

Pour toute commande supérieure à 500 F, Paris Foot vous offre le poster officiel de l'équipe.
(dans la limite du stock disponible)
Offre valable uniquement pour les commandes par correspondance.

Merci de votre commande
A chaque envoi, un nouveau bon de commande sera joint à votre colis.

Attention à la contrefaçon, ne vous laissez pas abuser par les vendeurs à la sauvette qui vous proposent des copies de nos produits officiels.

51 My Favourite Player (B): Task 1

INSTRUCTIONS: A player profile is provided below. Read it carefully, using the notes below if necessary.

FICHE
MON JOUEUR FAVORI

Nom: *Davy Jones*

Né: *le 2 mai 1975*

à: *Leytonminster*

Taille: *1,82 m*

Couleur des cheveux: *blonds*

Couleur des yeux: *bleus*

Poids: *75 kg*

Clubs successifs:
Manchester Wanderers
Preston Rovers

Poste: *milieu de terrain*

Nombre de buts en Championnat: *18*

Il est *doté d'une passe très précise et d'une frappe puissante*

C'est *un gros travailleur avec beaucoup de vitalité*

J'aime *son plaisir de jouer, et son intelligence*

Verdict: *Il donne tout. Un des meilleurs milieux de terrain de nos jours.*

NOTES

fiche	profile sheet	doté d'...	blessed with ...
nom	name	une passe très précise	a very accurate pass
né	date of birth	une frappe puissante	a powerful strike
à	place of birth	un gros travailleur	a hard worker
taille	height*	son plaisir de jouer	his love of the game
cheveux	hair	il donne tout	he gives it everything he's got
yeux	eyes	un des meilleurs	one of the best
poids	weight*	de nos jours	of our day
poste	position	il est ...	he is ...
milieu de terrain	midfield	c'est un ...	he's a ...
clubs successifs	clubs played for	j'aime	I like ...
nombre de buts	number of goals		
championnat	championship		

---

*
Height is measured in metres. In France, and in many other countries, a decimal point is shown not by a dot but by a comma. So **1,82m** is the same as **1.82m**.
Weight is always measured in kilogrammes, not stones and pounds.

51   My Favourite Player (B): Task 2

Prepare a profile like that in Task 1 for one of your own favourite players. A blank profile sheet is provided below, but you may prefer to make your own, particularly if you have other details to add. If you describe a female player you will need to change **Né** to **Née** and **Il est** to **Elle est**.

FICHE : MON JOUEUR FAVORI

Nom: _____

Né: _____

à: _____

Taille: _____

Poids: _____

Couleur des yeux: _____

Couleur des cheveux: _____

Poste: _____

Clubs successifs: _____

_____

Nombre de buts en Championnat: _____

Il est _____

C'est _____

J'aime _____

Verdict: _____

52 My Favourite Player (B): Task 2 - Study Sheet

Using an adjective to describe your player

Begin with the name of your player, or the pronoun **il** or **elle**. Read through the banks of expressions, noting those which seem to describe your player best. Use some of the words and expressions you have marked to complete your profile. When you have finished, make sure you know how to pronounce correctly any words you have chosen to use. Remember that if you are decribing a female player the adjective must be in the feminine form. Your teacher will help you with this if necessary. Help with describing playing positions etc. can be found elsewhere.

X est ...

	droitier	he's rightfooted
	gaucher	he's leftfooted
Il est ...	infatigable	he's tireless
	omniprésent	he seems to be everywhere at once
	clairvoyant	he's all seeing (has eyes in the back of his head)
	audacieux	he's bold / daring
	intraitable / intransigeant	he's uncompromising

(très)	athlétique	(very)	athletic
	adroit		skilful
	habile		skilful
	intelligent		intelligent
	ambitieux		ambitious
	assuré		confident
	régulier		consistent
	combatif		combative / a fighter
	tenace		persistent
	courageux		brave
	malin		sharp
	créatif		creative
	collectif		a team player
	calme		calm
	sûr		steady / reliable
	rapide		fast
	précis		accurate
	élégant		elegant
	opportuniste		ready to take any chance that's offered
	dynamique		dynamic
	patient		patient
	rigoureux		tough
	agressif		aggressive
	efficace		effective

Using a noun or noun phrase to describe your player

C'est un	bon frappeur des deux pieds	he can strike with either foot equally well
	gros travailleur	he's a hard worker
	marqueur de buts fabuleux	he's a scorer of fabulous goals
	tacleur extraordinaire	he's an extraordinary tackler
	buteur sans pareil	he's a striker without equal
	défenseur excellent	he's an excellent defender
	joueur très complet	he's a great all-rounder
	grand joueur	he's a great player
	technicien remarquable	he's an outstanding technician

C'est un	véritable génie du football	he's a real football genius
C'est une	vedette	he's a star

Saying what qualities your player has

Il a

beaucoup de vitalité	he has lots of energy
un sixième sense	he's got a sixth sense
du sang-froid	he keeps a cool head
d'excellents réflexes	he has sharp reflexes
une rare sûreté des mains	he handles the ball unusually well
un pied gauche impressionnant	he has an impressive left foot
une excellente vision du jeu	he reads the game well

Saying what it is you like about your player

J'aime

sa puissance physique	his strength
la rapidité de ses actions	his quick movements
son endurance	his stamina
son agilité	his agility
sa souplesse	his suppleness
sa coordination	his coordination
son contrôle du ballon	his ball control
sa vitesse de course	his speed
son plaisir de jouer	the way he enjoys playing
sa passion pour le jeu	his love of the game
sa bonne humeur	his good humour
sa combativité	his readiness to fight for the ball
son énergie	his energy
sa ténacité	his persistence
son sang-froid	his ability to keep a cool head
son sens du but	his feel for the goal
sa rapidité de décision	the speed with which he makes decisions
son marquage individuel	the way he marks his opponent
son jeu de tête	his headers
son habileté technique	his technical skill
son talent	his talent
sa concentration	his concentration
sa capacité d'anticiper une passe	his ability to anticipate a pass
sa capacité de duper son adversaire	his ability to deceive his opponent
sa capacité de frapper des deux pieds	his ability to kick with either foot equally well

Saying what impresses you about your player

You can construct a sentence beginning with one of the **son, sa, ses** phrases from the list above, followed by **est**, followed by one of the adjectives from the list below. (eg. Sa puissance physique est remarquable.) Remember that if you start with **Sa** the feminine form of the adjective will be needed. Adjectives which end in **e** are the same in either case.

remarquable	outstanding	spectaculaire	spectacular
extraordinaire	extraordinary	sans égal(e)	unequalled
magique	magic	sans pareil(le)	unmatched
intraitable	uncompromising	exceptionnel(le)	exceptional
légendaire	legendary	inné(e)	natural / inborn
formidable	terrific	impressionnant(e)	impressive
redoutable	formidable	excellent(e)	excellent
incroyable	unbelievable	évident(e)	obvious
très efficace	very effective	fabuleux (-euse)	fabulous

Finally, some superlatives (is your player the best, or one of the best?)

Use your dictionary if you are not sure of all the meanings

C'est	le meilleur	joueur		du monde
	le meilleur	buteur		sur la saison
	l'un des meilleurs	stoppeurs		de nos jours
		le joueur	le plus intelligent	de l'équipe

53 Newsletter

Bulletin

SUGGESTED ACTIVITIES:

- Use the Newsletter as a reading exercise.
- Create a True or False exercise.
- Write a letter in answer to the *Correspondants* or the *Petites Annonces*.

- Use it as a model for your desktop published version. Suggestions for items to include are given below (these are not necessarily translations of each other, but are included to suggest the flavour of a newsletter)

Prolongations	*Extra Time*
Petites Annonces	Small Ads
Correspondants	Penfriends
Interview d'une Star	Interview with a Star
24 heures avec....	24 hours with...
La Star du mois	Star of the Month
Le match du mois	Match of the Month
Le but du mois	Goal of the Month
L'équipe du mois	Team of the Month
Suspensions annoncées	Suspensions
Le saviez-vous..?	Did you know..?
Flash info	News Flash
Calendrier	Calendar of Events
Palmarès	Honours
Rétro - 1982 - cette année-là...	Retro - 1982 - that year...
Quelques euro chiffres	Vital Euro Statistics
Le shopping	In the Shops
Dessins des maillots	Football shirt designs
L'Histoire d'un Club	History of a Club
Des joueurs qui font de la publicité (shampooing etc)	Items advertised/endorsed by players (eg shampoo)
Courrier	Letters
Des trucs (de football)	Football tips
Des tuyaux	Inside Info
Sur le Web, Surfer le Web	On the Web, Surfing the Web
Poèmes	Poems
Les résultats	Results
Des photos	Photos
Echos	Gossip
La Mode des vedettes	Fashion of the stars
A à Z du Football	A-Z of football

Débat ou sondage - sur des questions d'actualité:
- *La commercialisation du sport - les prix des transfers, le prix des billets, le nombre et le coût des tenues, les sponsors*
- *Les hooligans, la drogue*
- *La forme et l'entraînement*
- *Nutrition et santé*
- *Motivation - le guérisseur!*
- *La sécurité pendant les matchs*
- *La conduite des joueurs sur et hors terrain*
- *Le nombre de fautes*

Debate or survey on topical issues:
- *The commercialisation of sport - transfer fees, cost of tickets, number and cost of kits, the role of the sponsors*
- *Football hooligans, drugs*
- *Fitness and training*
- *Nutrition and health*
- *Motivation - the Faith Healer!*
- *Safety at matches*
- *The conduct of players on and off the pitch*
- *The number of fouls*

PROLONGATIONS

Tête D'Affiche

Nom:	David Binkley
Né:	le 2 mai 1972
A:	Leytonstone
Taille:	1,82m
Poids:	75kg
Couleur des cheveux:	Noir
Couleur des yeux:	Brun
Musique favorite:	Salsa
Repas favori:	Pizza
Vacances favorites:	Le soleil, la plage, la natation
Poste:	Milieu de terrain
Clubs successifs:	Manchester Wanderers, Preston Town, Ipswich United
Nombre de buts en Championnat:	18
Il est:	Beau et athlétique!
J'adore:	Ses beaux yeux et ses cheveux!
Verdict:	*****C'est une vedette!

Manchester Wanderers: 0
Ipswich United: 2 (mi-temps: 0-1)

Samedi 28 février 1999

Coupe de la ligue

A:	Manchester
La Météo:	Il y avait du soleil
Stade:	Coronation Lane
Spectateurs:	50 000
Arbitre:	M. LeNoir
Buts:	Binkley (4e) et Noah (52e)
Avertissements:	Hildenberg (32e) et Jones (96e)
L'homme du match:	Binkley
On a aimé:	Son but fabuleux
On n'a pas aimé:	La faute de Jones
Verdict:	**** Un match sensationnel!

54 World Cup 2006 Teams (a)

Les équipes de la Coupe du Monde 2006 (a)

SUGGESTED LANGUAGE:

Pays + Couleurs (Maillot/Short/Bas)   *Country + Probable Colours (Shirt/Shorts/Socks)*

	Pays + Couleurs			*Country + Probable Colours*
1.	*Allemagne*	*blanc/noir/blancs*	1. Germany	white/black/white
2.	*Angleterre*	*blanc/bleu marine/blancs*	2. England	white/navy/white
3.	*Angola*	*rouge/noir/rouges*	3. Angola	red/black/red
4.	*Arabie Saoudite*	*blanc/vert/blancs*	4. Saudi Arabia	white/green/white
5.	*Argentine*	*bleu ciel-blanc/noir/blancs*	5. Argentina	blue-white/black/white
6.	*Australie*	*jaune/vert/jaunes*	6. Australia	yellow/green/yellow
7.	*Brésil*	*jaune/bleu/blancs*	7. Brasil	yellow/blue/white
8.	*Corée du Sud*	*rouge/noir/rouges*	8. South Korea	red/black/red
9.	*Costa Rica*	*rouge/bleu/blancs*	9. Costa Rica	red/blue/white
10.	*Côte d'Ivoire*	*vert/blanc/verts*	10. Ivory Coast	green/white/green
11.	*Croatie*	*rouge-blanc/blanc/bleus*	11. Croatia	red-white/white/blue
12.	*Equateur*	*jaune/bleu/rouges*	12. Ecuador	yellow/blue/red
13.	*Espagne*	*rouge/bleu/bleus*	13. Spain	red/blue/blue
14.	*Etats-Unis*	*blanc/bleu/blancs*	14. United States	white/blue/white
15.	*France*	*bleu/blanc/rouges*	15. France	blue/white/red
16.	*Ghana*	*blanc/blanc/blancs*	16. Ghana	white/white/white

ADDITIONAL LANGUAGE:

1.	*l'équipe allemande*	*the German team*
2.	*l'équipe anglaise*	*the English team*
3.	*l'équipe angolaise*	*the Angolan team*
4.	*l'équipe saoudienne*	*the Saudi team*
5.	*l'équipe argentine*	*the Argentinian team*
6.	*l'équipe australienne*	*the Australian team*
7.	*l'équipe brésilienne*	*the Brasilian team*
8.	*l'équipe sud-coréenne*	*the South Korean team*
9.	*l'équipe costaricaine*	*the Costa Rican team*
10.	*l'équipe ivoirienne*	*the Ivorian team*
11.	*l'équipe croate*	*the Croatian team*
12.	*l'équipe équatorienne*	*the Ecuador team*
13.	*l'équipe espagnole*	*the Spanish team*
14.	*l'équipe américaine*	*the American team*
15.	*l'équipe française*	*the French team*
16.	*l'équipe ghanéenne*	*the Ghanaian team*

SUGGESTED ACTIVITIES:

- Colour in the Kit according to the team colours above. You may like to check the final strip colours on the FIFA Website. Use in a wallchart for play-offs.
- Selected games from Unit 2, eg True or False, Bingo, Beat the Clock.
- Happy Families. Collect sets of players from different countries.
- Make DIY Dominoes or Matching Pairs with the Names of Countries and Teams.
- Betting Games: *Qui va gagner La Coupe du Monde? Who's going to win the World Cup?*
- Research information about the teams. Include in Newsletters or display in the Coin Football:

- Examples:

Fiches - Croatie:
Continent: *Europe*
Population: *4,7 millions*
Capitale: *Zagreb*
Couleurs: *Rouge, blanc et bleu*
Palmarès en Coupe du Monde: troisième en 1998

Angleterre:
Champion du Monde en 66, tour final en 1970 et 94, 2ème tour en 82, 4ème place en 90, quart de finale en 70 et 2002, huitième de finale en 86.

Allemagne	Angleterre	Angola	Arabie Saoudite
Argentine	Australie	Brésil	Corée du Sud
Costa Rica	Côte d'Ivoire	Croatie	Equateur
Espagne	Etats-Unis	France	Ghana

54 World Cup 2006 Teams (b)

Les équipes de la Coupe du Monde 2006 (b)

SUGGESTED LANGUAGE:

Pays + Couleurs (Maillot/Short/Bas)		*Country + Probable Colours (Shirt/Shorts/Socks)*	
17. Iran	blanc/blanc/blancs	Iran	white/white/white
18. Italie	bleu/blanc/bleus	Italy	blue/white/blue
19. Japon	bleu/blanc/bleus	Japan	blue/white/blue
20. Mexique	vert/blanc/rouges	Mexico	green/white/red
21. Paraguay	rouge-blanc/bleu/bleus	Paraguay	red-white/blue/blue
22. Pays-Bas	orange/blanc/orange	Holland	orange/white/orange
23. Pologne	blanc/rouge/blancs	Poland	white/red/white
24. Portugal	rouge/vert/rouges	Portugal	red/green/red
25. République tchèque	rouge/blanc/blancs	Czech Republic	red/white/white
26. Serbie-Monténégro	blanc/blanc/blancs	Serbia and Montenegro	white/white/white
27. Suède	jaune/bleu/jaunes	Sweden	yellow/blue/yellow
28. Suisse	rouge/blanc/rouges	Switzerland	red/white/red
29. Togo	jaune/vert/blancs	Togo	yellow/green/white
30. Trinité-et-Tobago	rouge/rouge/rouges	Trinidad and Tobago	red/red/red
31. Tunisie	rouge/blanc/rouges	Tunisia	red/white/red
32. Ukraine	jaune/jaune/jaunes	Ukraine	yellow/yellow/yellow

ADDITIONAL LANGUAGE:

17. l'équipe iranienne	the Iranian team
18. l'équipe italienne	the Italian team
19. l'équipe japonaise	the Japanese team
20. l'équipe mexicaine	the Mexican team
21. l'équipe paraguayenne	the Paraguayan team
22. l'équipe hollandaise	the Dutch team
23. l'équipe polonaise	the Polish team
24. l'équipe portugaise	the Portuguese team
25. l'équipe tchèque	the Czech team
26. l'équipe serbo-monténégrine	the Serbian and Montenegro team
27. l'équipe suédoise	the Swedish team
28. l'équipe suisse	the Swiss team
29. l'équipe togolaise	the Togolese team
30. l'équipe de la Trinité	the Trinidad and Tobago (T&T) team
31. l'équipe tunisienne	the Tunisian team
32. l'équipe ukrainienne	the Ukrainian team

SUGGESTED ACTIVITIES:

- See previous page.

55a and 55b 2006 World Cup Teams - Flags

(NB These are artist's impressions of the flags.)

SUGGESTED ACTIVITIES:

- Look up the flags using an encyclopedia, or the web, and colour them in.
- Look up the countries pinpointed on the world map on the FIFA Website.
- Place them on a classroom world map.
- Selected activities from Unit 2, eg Odd One Out (colours, continents), True or False, Guessing Game, Bingo, Happy Families
- Cut out and play Dominoes or Matching Pairs with the Names of Countries and Flags. Reminder: with dominoes, make sure the matching sides are not on the same domino!

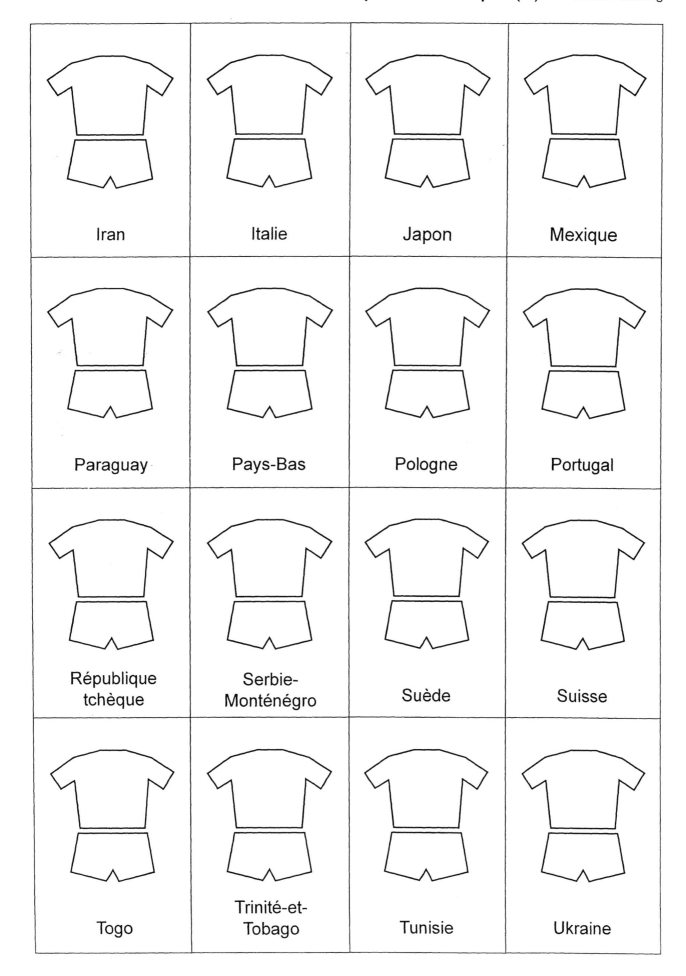

Iran	Italie	Japon	Mexique
Paraguay	Pays-Bas	Pologne	Portugal
République tchèque	Serbie-Monténégro	Suède	Suisse
Togo	Trinité-et-Tobago	Tunisie	Ukraine

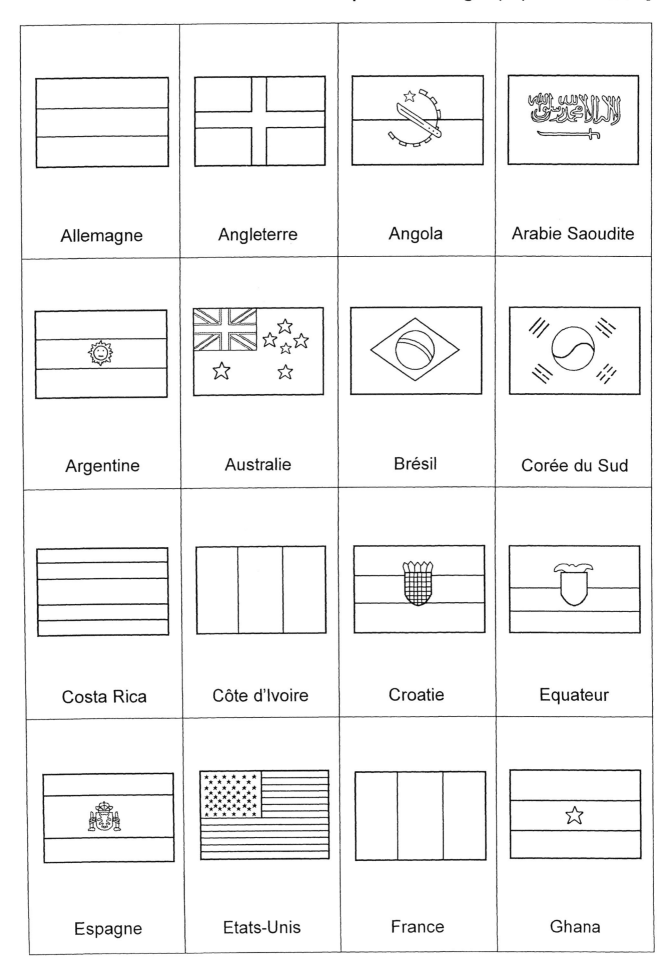

Allemagne	Angleterre	Angola	Arabie Saoudite
Argentine	Australie	Brésil	Corée du Sud
Costa Rica	Côte d'Ivoire	Croatie	Equateur
Espagne	Etats-Unis	France	Ghana

Iran	Italie	Japon	Mexique
Paraguay	Pays-Bas	Pologne	Portugal
République tchèque	Serbie-Monténégro	Suède	Suisse
Togo	Trinité-et-Tobago	Tunisie	Ukraine

55 2006 World Cup Flag Dominoes (bi)

©MLG

Flag	Name	Flag	Name
	Allemagne		Costa Rica
	Angleterre		Côte d'Ivoire
	Angola		Croatie
	Arabie Saoudite		Equateur
	Argentine		Espagne
	Australie		Etats-Unis
	Brésil		France
	Corée du Sud		Ghana

55   2006 World Cup Flag Dominoes (bii)

©MLG

Iran		République tchèque		
Italie		Serbie-Monténégro		
Japon		Suède		
Mexique		Suisse		
Paraguay		Togo		
Pays-Bas		Trinité-et-Tobago		
Pologne		Tunisie		
Portugal		Ukraine		

56 2006 World Cup Stadia

SUGGESTED LANGUAGE:

Berlin	Hanovre
Cologne	Kaiserslautern
Dortmund	Leipzig
Francfort	Munich
Gelsenkirchen	Nuremberg
Hambourg	Stuttgart

SUGGESTED ACTIVITIES:

- Look up the names of the towns on a map of Germany.
- Write the names of the cities/towns on the map and enlarge the map for display in the Coin Football.
- Put daily weather symbols on the map.
- Look up the FIFA website (given in several languages), describe the situation of a stadium and give other details about it.
- Examples:

Hambourg

Situation: Au nord-ouest de l'Allemagne
Population: 1,7 million
Stade: Stade de la Coupe du Monde de la FIFA de Hambourg
Projet: Stade entièrement neuf
Coût : 97 millions Euro
Capacité brute: 51 055
Total places assises: 45 442
Places disponibles à la vente   1er Tour: 40 918
Quarts de finale: 40 226

Berlin

Situation: Au nord-est de l'Allemagne
Population: 3,39 millions
Stade: Olympiastadion

Projet: Reconstruction
Coût : 242 millions Euro
Capacité brute: 74,220
Total places assises: 66 021
Places disponibles à la vente Premier tour: 56 358
Quarts de finale: 56 316   Finale: 55 562

Use the FIFA website to calculate the distance between stadia and how to get there:

Quelle est la distance exacte entre Munich et Hambourg? Ou de Dortmund à Leipzig? En entrant tout simplement votre point de départ et votre point d'arrivée, les distances sont affichées en une fraction de seconde. De plus, un menu déroulant vous propose une série de destinations intéressantes, de façon à vous faire gagner du temps.

De: **Gelsenkirchen** à Hanovre   Distance: **233.1 km**   Durée du trajet en voiture: **2 heures 15 minutes**

Research more information:

Actualités, La ville, Le stade, Galerie de Photos, Vidéo, Distances, Transports publics, Aller au stade
Infos trafic, Plans des villes, Services d'Hébergement

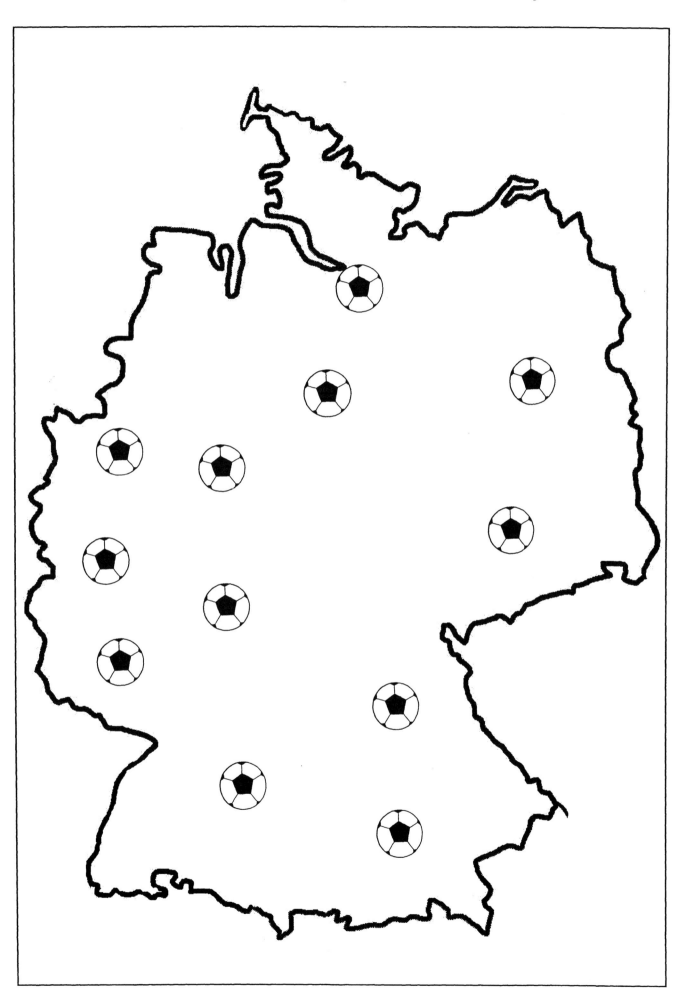

57 2006 World Cup Fixtures – Ist Round

Learners could fill in the results for each match. They could then draw up charts for the next rounds eg:
8e de finale, quart de finale, demi-finale, finale
Finale 3e et 4e Place – Perdant 1 et Perdant 2
Finale 1re et 2e Place – Vainqueur 1 et Vainqueur 2

58 2006 World Cup Groups

Groupe A	Allemagne Costa Rica Pologne Equateur	Groupe E	Italie Ghana Etats-Unis République tchèque
Groupe B	Angleterre Paraguay Trinité-et-Tobago Suède	Groupe F	Brésil Croatie Australie Japon
Groupe C	Argentine Côte d'Ivoire Serbie-Monténégro Pays-Bas	Groupe G	France Suisse Corée du Sud Togo
Groupe D	Mexique Iran Angola Portugal	Groupe H	Espagne Ukraine Tunisie Arabie Saoudite

SUGGESTED ACTIVITY:

- Happy Families. See following pages. Play in the usual way, collecting teams in eg Group A or Group D.

Villes / Juin	Stuttgart	Nuremberg	Munich	Leipzig	Kaisers-lautern	Hanovre	Hambourg	Gelsen-kirchen	Francfort	Dortmund	Cologne	Berlin
Ven-09			Allemagne - Costa Rica 01 18H00					Pologne - Equateur 02 21H00				
Sam-10							Argentine - Côte d'Ivoire 05 21H00		Angleterre - Paraguay 03 15H00	Trin et Tob - Suède 04 18H00	Angola - Portugal 08 21H00	
Dim-11		Mexique - Iran 07 18H00		Serbie-Mont - Pays-Bas 06 15H00								
Lun-12					Australie - Japon 12 15H00	Italie - Ghana 09 21H00		Etats-Unis - Rép tchèque 10 18H00				
Mar-13	France - Suisse 13 18H00								Cor de Sud - Togo 14 15H00			Brésil - Croatie 11 21H00
Mer-14			Tunisie - Arabie Saou 16 18H00	Espagne - Ukraine 15 15H00						Allemagne - Pologne 17 21H00		
Jeu-15		Angleterre - Trin et Tob 19 18H00					Equateur - Costa Rica 18 15H00					Suède - Paraguay 20 21H00
Ven-16	Pays-Bas - Côte d'Ivoire 22 18H00					Mexique - Angola 23 21H00		Argentine - Serbie-Mont 21 15H00				
Sam-17					Italie - Etats-Unis 25 21H00				Portugal - Iran 24 15H00		Rép tchèque - Ghana 26 18H00	
Dim-18		Japon - Croatie 28 15H00	Brésil - Australie 27 18H00	France - Corée du Sud 29 21H00								
Lun-19	Espagne - Tunisie 31 21H00						Arabie Saou - Ukraine 32 18H00			Togo - Suisse 30 15H00		
Mar-20					Paraguay - Trin et Tob 36 21H00	Costa Rica - Pologne 34 16H00					Suède - Angleterre 35 21H00	Equateur - Allemagne 33 16H00
Mer-21			Côte d'Ivoire - Serbie-Mont 38 21H00	Iran - Angola 40 16H00				Portugal - Mexique 39 16H00	Pays-Bas - Argentine 37 21H00			
Jeu-22	Croatie - Australie 44 21H00	Ghana - Etats-Unis 42 16H00					Rép tchèque - Italie 41 16H00			Japon - Brésil 43 21H00		
Ven-23					Arabie Saou - Espagne 47 16H00	Suisse - Corée du Sud 46 21H00					Togo - France 45 21H00	Ukraine - Tunisie 48 16H00

Groupe A	**Groupe A**	**Groupe A**	**Groupe A**
Allemagne	*Allemagne*	*Allemagne*	*Allemagne*
Costa Rica	**Costa Rica**	*Costa Rica*	*Costa Rica*
Pologne	*Pologne*	**Pologne**	*Pologne*
Equateur	*Equateur*	*Equateur*	**Equateur**

Groupe B	**Groupe B**	**Groupe B**	**Groupe B**
Angleterre	*Angleterre*	*Angleterre*	*Angleterre*
Paraguay	**Paraguay**	*Paraguay*	*Paraguay*
Trinité-et-Tobago	*Trinité-et-Tobago*	**Trinité-et-Tobago**	*Trinité-et-Tobago*
Suède	*Suède*	*Suède*	**Suède**

Groupe C	**Groupe C**	**Groupe C**	**Groupe C**
Argentine	*Argentine*	*Argentine*	*Argentine*
Côte d'Ivoire	**Côte d'Ivoire**	*Côte d'Ivoire*	*Côte d'Ivoire*
Serbie-Monténégro	*Serbie-Monténégro*	**Serbie-Monténégro**	*Serbie-Monténégro*
Pays-Bas	*Pays-Bas*	*Pays-Bas*	**Pays-Bas**

Groupe D	**Groupe D**	**Groupe D**	**Groupe D**
Mexique	*Mexique*	*Mexique*	*Mexique*
Iran	**Iran**	*Iran*	*Iran*
Angola	*Angola*	**Angola**	*Angola*
Portugal	*Portugal*	*Portugal*	**Portugal**

Groupe E	**Groupe E**	**Groupe E**	**Groupe E**
Italie	*Italie*	*Italie*	*Italie*
Ghana	**Ghana**	*Ghana*	*Ghana*
Etats-Unis	*Etats-Unis*	**Etats-Unis**	*Etats-Unis*
République tchèque	*République tchèque*	*République tchèque*	**République tchèque**

Groupe F	**Groupe F**	**Groupe F**	**Groupe F**
Brésil	*Brésil*	*Brésil*	*Brésil*
Croatie	**Croatie**	*Croatie*	*Croatie*
Australie	*Australie*	**Australie**	*Australie*
Japon	*Japon*	*Japon*	**Japon**

Groupe G	**Groupe G**	**Groupe G**	**Groupe G**
France	*France*	*France*	*France*
Suisse	**Suisse**	*Suisse*	*Suisse*
Corée du Sud	*Corée du Sud*	**Corée du Sud**	*Corée du Sud*
Togo	*Togo*	*Togo*	**Togo**

Groupe H	**Groupe H**	**Groupe H**	**Groupe H**
Espagne	*Espagne*	*Espagne*	*Espagne*
Ukraine	**Ukraine**	*Ukraine*	*Ukraine*
Tunisie	*Tunisie*	**Tunisie**	*Tunisie*
Arabie Saoudite	*Arabie Saoudite*	*Arabie Saoudite*	**Arabie Saoudite**

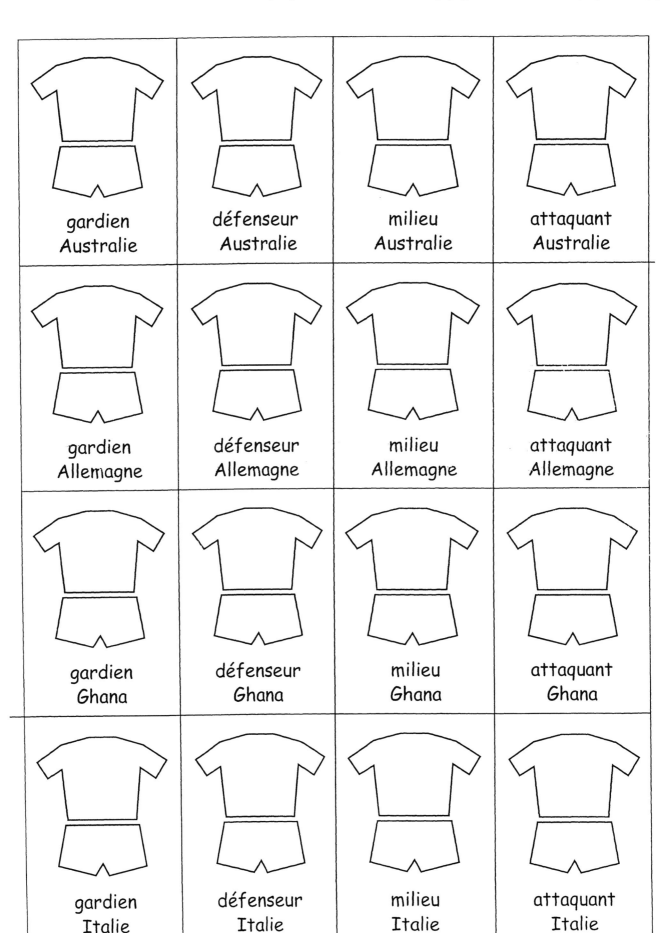

| gardien | défenseur | milieu | attaquant |
| Australie | Australie | Australie | Australie |

| gardien | défenseur | milieu | attaquant |
| Allemagne | Allemagne | Allemagne | Allemagne |

| gardien | défenseur | milieu | attaquant |
| Ghana | Ghana | Ghana | Ghana |

| gardien | défenseur | milieu | attaquant |
| Italie | Italie | Italie | Italie |

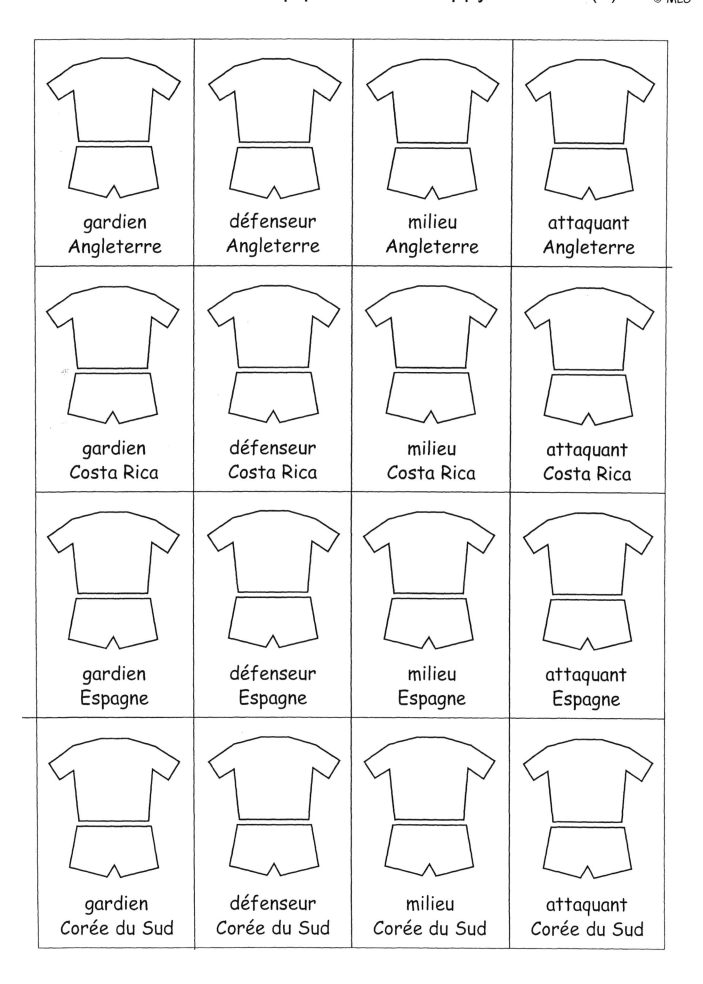

gardien Angleterre	défenseur Angleterre	milieu Angleterre	attaquant Angleterre
gardien Costa Rica	défenseur Costa Rica	milieu Costa Rica	attaquant Costa Rica
gardien Espagne	défenseur Espagne	milieu Espagne	attaquant Espagne
gardien Corée du Sud	défenseur Corée du Sud	milieu Corée du Sud	attaquant Corée du Sud

60   Les Équipes

The French names of thirty of the countries playing in the 1998 World Cup are hidden in the grid below. Find them, mark them then write them in the spaces provided.

```
Ê  A  I  T  A  L  I  E  G  È  V  R  O  N  B
F  R  P  Z  J  A  U  É  S  S  O  C  É  E  R
J  A  M  A  ï  Q  U  E  É  P  L  Ô  N  U  É
I  B  L  É  I  Q  I  T  I  R  A  N  V  Q  S
Ç  I  Z  L  I  N  E  Ê  R  B  O  G  A  I  I
Q  E  I  R  A  G  L  U  B  I  M  C  N  X  L
V  H  F  M  A  R  O  C  Q  H  C  O  G  E  T
C  A  U  P  C  F  G  I  P  I  B  H  L  M  Î
C  O  É  Ç  A  L  L  E  M  A  G  N  E  O  E
R  Q  É  Y  M  R  A  L  N  Î  P  L  T  X  C
O  D  A  N  E  M  A  R  K  T  Q  Ç  E  E  N
A  L  Ï  Î  R  N  I  G  É  R  I  A  R  B  A
T  C  A  N  O  P  A  J  U  K  W  N  R  M  R
I  B  Y  O  U  G  O  S  L  A  V  I  E  H  F
E  Î  T  U  N  I  S  I  E  L  Y  C  V  P  V
```

1 _____ du Sud
2 _____ du Sud
3 _____ Saoudite
4 _____
5 _____
6 _____
7 _____
8 _____
9 _____
10 _____
11 _____
12 _____
13 _____
14 _____
15 _____
16 _____
17 _____
18 _____
19 _____
20 _____
21 _____
22 _____
23 _____
24 _____
25 _____
26 _____
27 _____
28 _____
29 _____
30 _____

**Two of the competing teams are missing from the grid.
Which are they?
Write their names below (in French, if possible!).**

Team 31 _____   Team 32 _____

© Miniflashcards Language Games

Le Football (A)

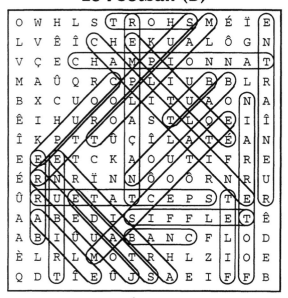

Le Football (B)

Les Équipes

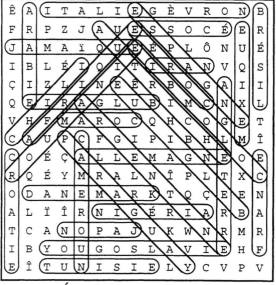

Team 31: ÉTATS-UNIS. Team 32: PAYS-BAS.

PARTICIPATING TEAMS	
French	English
AFRIQUE (du Sud) … …South Africa
ALLEMAGNE … … … … …Germany
ANGLETERRE … … … … …England
ARABIE (Saoudite) … …Saudi Arabia
ARGENTINE … … … … …Argentia
AUTRICHE … … … … … …Austria
BELGIQUE … … … … … …Belgium
BRÉSIL … … … … … … …Brazil
BULGARIE … … … … … …Bulgaria
CAMEROUN … … … … …Cameroon
CHILI … … … … … … … …Chile
COLOMBIE … … … … …Columbia
CORÉE (du Sud) … … …South Korea
CROATIE … … … … … … …Croatia
DANEMARK … … … … …Denmark
ÉCOSSE … … … … … … …Scotland
ESPAGNE … … … … … … …Spain
ÉTATS-UNIS … … … …United States
FRANCE … … … … … … …France
IRAN … … … … … … … …Iran
ITALIE … … … … … … … …Italy
JAMAïQUE … … … … … …Jamaica
JAPON … … … … … … …Japan
MAROC … … … … … … …Morocco
MEXIQUE … … … … … …Mexico
NIGÉRIA … … … … … …Nigeria
NORVÈGE … … … … … …Norway
PARAGUAY … … … … …Paraguay
PAYS-BAS … … … … … …Holland
ROUMANIE … … … … …Rumania
TUNISIE … … … … … … …Tunisia
YOUGOSLAVIE … … … …Yugoslavia

61   Templates

Examples are provided of the following:

- Tick Grid
- Snakes and Ladders
- 9 Picture Grid
- 12 Picture Grid
- Football Kits

Tick grid

Snakes and ladders

©MLG

50	49	48	47	46
41	42	43	44	45
40	39	38	37	36
31	32	33	34	35
30	29	28	27	26
21	22	23	24	25
20	19	18	17	16
11	12	13	14	15
10	9	8	7	6
1	2	3	4	5

9 card grid

12 card grid

© MLG

Template

© MLG